I have known Renee and her husband Allen for many years—she is a wonderful mum to three gorgeous girls and has a heartfelt desire to build into the lives of others. Her devotion to all things true and pure is no small thing, and I love that she has taken the time to compose this book and bring her passion to life within its pages. I trust her guidance on this topic will enrich the marriage of every reader and help you cultivate a profound relationship with your spouse.

Bobbie Houston
Co-Global Senior Pastor, Hillsong Church

This book is a timely and valuable resource for both Christian and non-Christian couples. While written from a Biblical perspective, the advice and techniques described and explained are valuable for couples, whether just engaged or in a long-term married relationship. I particularly like the fact that the book emphasizes intimacy and communication while not avoiding the nitty gritty of physical sex.

On a more personal note, I have followed the author Renee's development from a postgraduate student through to a practicing sexologist. It gives me great pleasure to endorse this book.

Dr Patricia Weerakoon
Sexologist, Author, Speaker

It's my pleasure to endorse this book by author Renee Yam. I've known Renee for about ten years. Her passion to help people, combined with her knowledge in the field of sexology, has led to the writing of this current book. I have no doubt this will be the first of many. *Sex Awakened* draws together Renee's clinical experience and studies into a text that is both informative and practical. That combination is where its benefits lie, as a book for couples to read and re-read over the course of their married lives. Renee marries her Christian world view into this book, which perhaps may limit the readership, but I would endorse it to all heterosexual couples who value long term vibrant healthy relationships.

Dr Jo Thomas
General Practitioner, Sydney

Renee Yam in her book, *Sex Awakened* encourages newlyweds to discover what the bible says about sexual intimacy and how to have a healthy sex life within their marriage. She shares her insights in an informed and practical manner. Renee's commitment to seeing Christians flourish in their relationships is inspiring and refreshing.

Margaret Aghajanian
National Pastoral Care Oversight
Hillsong Church Australia

SEX AWAKENED

Cultivating healthy sexual
intimacy in marriage

Copyright © 2020 by Renee Yam

All rights reserved. No part of this publication may be reproduced, distributed, or transmitted in any form or by any means, including photocopying, recording, or other electronic or mechanical methods, without the prior written permission of the publisher.

ISBN Softcover: 978-0-6488529-0-2
ISBN Kindle: 978-0-6488529-1-9

Scripture quotations marked (NLT) are taken from the Holy Bible, New Living Translation, copyright ©1996, 2004, 2015 by Tyndale House Foundation. Used by permission of Tyndale House Publishers, a Division of Tyndale House Ministries, Carol Stream, Illinois 60188. All rights reserved.

Scripture marked (MSG) are taken from The Message. Copyright © 1993, 1994, 1995, 1996, 2000, 2001, 2002. Used by permission of NavPress Publishing Group.

Scripture quotations marked TPT are from The Passion Translation®. Copyright © 2017, 2018 by Passion & Fire Ministries, Inc. Used by permission. All rights reserved. ThePassionTranslation.com.

Scripture quotations marked (AMP) are taken from the Amplified Bible, Copyright © 1954, 1958, 1962, 1964, 1965, 1987 by The Lockman Foundation. Used by permission.

Scripture quotations marked (NIV) are taken from the Holy Bible, New International Version®, NIV®. Copyright © 1973, 1978, 1984, 2011 by Biblica, Inc.™ Used by permission of Zondervan. All rights reserved worldwide.

Cover photograph: @bantersnaps on Unsplash
Cover Models: Jennae Woyen, Gage Woyen
Editing and pre-production: Torn Curtain Publishing

Published by Sex, The Whole Story
Sydney, Australia
www.sexthewholestory.com.au

A catalogue record of this book is available from the National Library of Australia

SEX AWAKENED

Cultivating healthy sexual
intimacy in marriage

RENEE YAM

CONTENTS

    INTRODUCTION   9

1. THE GOD OF INTIMACY   11
   Discovering your Creator's purpose and plan for sex

2. THE POWER OF SEX   33
   Understanding your brain, body and sexual desire

3. THE BEAUTY AND WONDER OF YOUR SEXUALITY   67
   Embracing the gift of physical intimacy

4. YOUR PRIVATE PARADISE   83
   Awakening and exploring pleasure in intimacy

5. SEX CHATS   117
   Developing your most powerful sexual technique

6. YOUR SEXUAL JOURNEY   135
   Cultivating great sex together

7. HONOUR YOUR INTIMACY   151
   Safeguarding your sex life

INTRODUCTION

I am so pleased that you have picked up this book. Congratulations! The fact that you are reading this right now shows your desire to be equipped with knowledge that you can invest into your most intimate relationship, your marriage.

The relationships in our lives are vital to our personal wellbeing, and how we do them is so important. Think of your relationship with God, with yourself, and with your spouse, your children, your family, and friends; how we relate matters! Each relationship has the potential to enrich our lives, to give our lives purpose and deep meaning. That is because we have an innate wiring for connection. We are designed for relationship.

Despite the fact that our relationships play such a critical role in our personal wellbeing, the reality is that we don't always know how to do them well. So often, we simply adopt the patterns that have been handed to us, and if these dynamics are not healthy, they not only affect our own relationships, but they in turn become what we pass down to the next generation. Those relationships certainly have the ability to build us up and makes us better, but they also have the power to tear us down. We therefore need to learn how to cultivate healthy and respectful relationships, to be the best we can be, both for ourselves and others.

This book focuses on healthy sexual intimacy within God-designed covenant marriages. Our sexuality is such an essential part of our lives—and yet, our sexuality is complex. Our culture and the society we are raised in, have a profound influence on our understanding, as do the many experiences we carry from our childhood, adolescence and even our adult lives.

Our sexuality is intrinsically connected to our physical, mental, emotional *and* spiritual wellbeing. How we think and feel about our sexuality, how comfortable we are with our body, how we express love and affection, and what we believe in terms of our faith, are all connected to our sexual expression. It is so important, therefore, that we approach our sexuality from a holistic perspective in order to better understand ourselves and how we relate to others, and so we can enjoy sexually positive and healthy marriages.

As an engaged or newly married couple, or even as an individual who would like to deepen your understanding of sex, my hope for this book is that it equips you with knowledge and understanding about what holistic, healthy sexual intimacy can look like within a God-designed and God-honouring marriage. As you work through each chapter, I encourage you to consider your personal beliefs, values and attitudes towards sex. You will find that this book is packed with healthy insights into holistic sexuality as well as practical ways to enhance sexual intimacy in your marriage. Enjoy!

1.
THE GOD OF INTIMACY

Discovering your Creator's purpose
and plan for sex

> *'Deep within us all is a desire to be close to another,
> to be known and to be loved.'*

God is the God of intimacy. He is one God that eternally exists as three distinct persons—the Father, Son and Holy Spirit. Each are equal in all their qualities; they exist in unity and they relate to each other personally. They are intimately known by each other. Each is fully God, and all three persons are the same God. They constitute the one true God, creator of Heaven and Earth.

Before the foundation of the world, God was in fellowship with himself! Father, Son and Holy Spirit have always existed in beautiful relationship with one another. God is not, and never was, lonely. He is always in intimacy. God is an intimate and personal God.

YOU ARE CREATED FOR INTIMACY

> *'Then God said, "Let us make human beings in our image, to be like us. They will reign over the fish in the sea, the birds in the sky, the livestock, all the wild animals on the earth, and the small animals that scurry along the ground."'*
> *Genesis 1.26 NLT*

God created us in His image, in the image of the Trinity, therefore, we too, are created for intimacy! We have a need to be known by another. This need to be close, affirmed and loved drives us into relationship. We are relational beings, wired for intimacy with God and others.

As human beings, we not only crave connection, but we flourish and thrive in relationships. Intimacy is letting another person really see you. It is sharing *who you really are* with someone else. Intimacy is about being known, deeply known.

There are four elements of intimacy: to belong to someone, to be known by that person, to be affirmed, and ultimately, to be accepted.

> *When you belong to someone, you have a place.*
> *When you are known by someone, you are seen.*
> *When you are affirmed by someone, you are validated.*
> *When you are accepted by someone, you are enough.*

When we belong, and are known, affirmed and accepted, we receive the liberty and courage to reveal more of ourselves to another. We are able to drop our guard a little more, to give ourselves permission to be real and raw. We get to be our authentic and genuine selves with another person!

This liberty allows us to let go of ourselves, to be silly, playful and fun. It creates safety within the relationship, enabling us to be brave and courageous, to make mistakes, and to experience failure and success. Intimacy is the courageous relational journey of revealing more of yourself to another, and it needs to be met with belonging, affirmation and acceptance.

Like an onion, intimacy has many layers; as each layer is peeled back, we are brought closer to the core. Likewise, in our relationships, when our layers are peeled back, more of who we are is revealed to each other. There is so much to know about another person!

The more we reveal about ourselves and the more we know about someone else, the closer and more intimate our relationship grows. And whenever revealing is met with belonging, affirmation and acceptance, there is an opportunity for healing, wholeness and restoration to be experienced as we are built up and validated. Intimacy is healing!

Intimacy with God

God longs for you to bond intimately with Him, to find Him irresistible. We are created to bond deeply to God! The perfect love that comes from an intimate relationship with God makes us sufficient, secure and whole.

This is the most important relationship we are created to have. God is the only one who can meet all our needs. God is the only one who makes us complete.

Intimacy with Others

Our main relationships are outworked in families, communities and friendships. We are better together! The belonging, support and encouragement we receive from being in relationship enhances our lives and gives us a beautiful sense of purpose and satisfaction.

Our lives are enriched when our relationships are healthy and flourishing. Intimacy, however, goes further than that. Intimacy is letting another person really see you. It is sharing who you really are. Intimacy is being *known* on all levels—emotionally, mentally, physically, spiritually and sexually.

The closeness experienced through intimacy allows us to experience the fullness of each other.

Intimacy in Marriage

Marriage has the potential to be the most intimate relationship we ever have. A marriage where two people can be known emotionally, mentally, physically, spiritually and sexually, is a beautiful and sacred relationship. And since there are layers and layers of 'knowing someone' in marriage, it is important to remember that intimacy in marriage is far more than just the act of sex.

First of all, intimacy is *spiritual*.

It is about sharing your spiritual encounters, revelations, or moments with God together.

> **Talk it over:**
>
> *As a couple, do you pray together? Worship together? Do bible devotions together? Do you share what God is doing in your hearts? Do you talk about your God-dreams and passions?*

Secondly, intimacy is *recreational*.

It is creating beautiful moments, sharing new experiences, and making memories together. It may be going for an evening stroll or travelling and discovering new places together.

> **Chat together:**
>
> *What activities do you enjoy together? What new experiences or new things do you try together? Do you laugh and have fun in each other's presence?*

Thirdly, intimacy is *intellectual*.

It's about sharing your thoughts, ideas, and the things that you care about, with each other.

> **Ask yourselves:**
>
> *Do you discuss, debate, and explore various topics together? Do you know how each other thinks about the issues of life? Do you know what each other's values are, and why those values hold meaning for your spouse?*

Fourthly, intimacy is *physical*.

It is about connecting and comforting each other through physical touch—like massages, hugs, kisses, and holding hands. It's about the consistent, daily, non-sexual physical affection you offer each other.

> **Take a moment to discuss:**
>
> *How affectionate are you towards each other? How does it feel to you when you are physically close to each other?*

Fifthly, intimacy is *emotional*.

It requires being honest and open with each other as you share your joy and happiness, as well as your fears, pain and tears.

> **Know each other:**
>
> *Do you share your personal experiences and emotions with each other? Can you identify with each other's feelings? What matters most to your partner—and why? What hurts them? What fills them with passion and fire?*

Lastly, intimacy is *sexual* — and that is what this book is about! But as you can see, sexual intimacy is just *one* way of experiencing intimacy in your marriage.

INTIMACY IS BUILT

Intimacy in every relationship, whether it is with God, others, or your spouse, requires intentional investment. Intimacy does not just happen! It is built — purposefully. Think for a moment. Who can you be yourself around? Who can you freely let yourself go with? Who do you allow close enough to know you deeply?

The four key ingredients for building intimacy are: trust, safety, respect and vulnerability; each one is essential if we are to experience healthy, life-giving relationships:

Trust

'I am here for you . . . and I will protect you.'

Trust is built in the small decisions and seemingly insignificant moments of life, and often it is conveyed most clearly when a person simply 'shows up' for you.

Trust is physical. It brings the assurance that, 'I will not walk away from you, I will not give myself to anyone else, I will stand by your side through the good, the bad and the ugly, and whatever may come our way, I choose you.' Trust allows a person to know that there will always be someone in their corner.

Trust is also emotional. 'I trust you will listen to me, that you will keep my most private thoughts to yourself, that you will not talk about me behind my back, that you will do what you say you will do.' Trust says, 'I know that you will see me when I'm sad, or confused, or down, that you will notice me . . . that you will stop to enquire how I am.'

Trust is built when people show they care, when they take the time to listen to what the other says because they desire to know their heart and intention. Trust is crucial if a couple is to truly be vulnerable with one another.

Safety

'You are my safe place. I can be myself around you, knowing I won't be judged.'

Human beings are innately wired to move away from danger and towards safety—even in relationships. Safety in relationship, therefore, is being free from danger, injury and loss, both physically and emotionally. Safety means you can speak up, that you can voice your opinion knowing that you will be heard, validated and affirmed. Safety involves knowing that your partner has your best interests at heart, that through their words and actions they demonstrate that you are their priority—that you are the most important person to them.

A safe relationship comes with a healthy supply of encouragement, support, comfort and nourishment, along with room for each individual to grow and flourish. In a safe marriage, you get to be each other's biggest cheerleader! There is honesty and truthfulness in your relationship. You each take responsibility for your own actions, feelings and behaviour, apologising when you are in the wrong, and being willing to make amends.

Safety comes when both partners in a relationship are reliable, consistent and accountable, and where control, criticism, judgement, neglect, pressure, and casting blame to avoid personal responsibility are not present—and not accepted.

Respect

'I feel respected because I am treated with worth and dignity.'

Respect is where both partners' voices and opinions, privacy, personal needs, time, unique identity, and personality are valued. Respect means treating each other equally, honouring each other in the way you speak. It means refusing to put your partner down or make jokes at their expense. Respect means not humiliating or treating your spouse in a dishonouring or unappreciative way. Instead, respect recognises the 'gold' within your partner, the potential they carry; it values who they are as a unique individual. Remember, both of you are equal in your worth!

When it comes to your partner's beliefs and values, respect means you do not try to change them or control them for your own personal benefit. Respect honours a person's choice and gives them the freedom to decide for themselves. It honours the personal space and boundaries around another person.

Respect also invites open communication; it enables you to discuss feelings and differences with a desire to understand each other's point of view. It ensures you make decisions together, having thoughtfully considered the needs of both people. When compromises are made for the sake of the relationship, you don't have to lose out or stop being yourself! Your own passions, interests, talent or career, and even your social life, can still flourish.

In the end, a relationship that upholds respect for one another is free from manipulation, pressure, intimidation, domination, and unrealistic and unhealthy expectations. It leaves both people free to fully be themselves.

Vulnerability

'I can be courageously vulnerable with you because you met me in my vulnerable place with love and acceptance. I am not alone with you.'

Vulnerability is risky and emotionally exposing because it enables your partner to know your fears and insecurities, your hopes and dreams. It means sharing your deepest feelings and emotions. It involves revealing parts of you that no one else may know about. And, it means sharing not only your successes and celebrations, but your experiences of embarrassment, missed opportunities and failure.

Vulnerability is scary because it is uncertain how people will respond. Will they laugh with you—or at you? Will they reject you, or will they join you and sit together with you in your fears and insecurities? Will they hold you when your pain is exposed? Will they love you in your shortcomings? Will they believe you can achieve the dreams you shared? Will they feel the same for you as you feel for them? As researcher Brené Brown so aptly says in her book, 'Daring Greatly': *Vulnerability sounds like truth and feels like courage.*[1]

It can be incredibly healing to be fully known by another, but it requires your time, your communication, your gentleness, your generosity, your kindness, and your intentional decision to show up and be present with your spouse. So be a person your spouse can trust! Be the safe place they can run to and rely on. Give them honour and respect for who they are as a unique individual with great worth, and decide to live vulnerably, opening up and sharing your whole self with them.

---

[1] B Brown, Daring Greatly: How the courage to be vulnerable transforms the way we live, love, parent, and lead, published by Avery, 2015

If we are not growing closer together and building a sense of connection between each other, we are actually doing the opposite — how easily we can grow apart, becoming less connected, less dependent, and less bonded. This breeds independence. Simply by doing nothing, we become less intimate with each other. In our marriage, then, we are doing either one or the other!

Let's never forget that intimacy is built in the small, daily moments when couples choose to turn towards each other, to be present and to connect with each other. It is in those unglamorous, everyday interactions that you can make your partner feel like they are the only person in the world that matters. And *that* is intimacy.

GOD'S PLAN FOR SEXUAL INTIMACY

Sex is a wonderful, joyful, self-giving and pleasurable experience, a celebration of two people's love for each other. Sex is also for procreation. Out of a beautiful, fulfilling, committed relationship, sex is designed as a means of reproducing your love for each other, building generations, and creating families of disciples.

> 'Then the Lord God said, "It is not good for the man to be alone. I will make a helper who is just right for him . . . Let us make human beings in our image, to be like us . . ." So God created human beings in his own image. In the image of God, he created them; male and female he created them. Then God blessed them and said, "Be fruitful and multiply."'
> Genesis 2.18, 1:26-28 NLT

Sex is also for unity; it bonds a man and a woman together in oneness and deep intimacy at an emotional, physical and spiritual level.

> 'While the man slept, the Lord God took out one of the man's ribs and closed up the opening. Then the Lord God made a

> woman from the rib, and he brought her to the man. "At last!" the man exclaimed. "This one is bone from my bone, and flesh from my flesh! She will be called 'woman,' because she was taken from 'man.'" This explains why a man leaves his father and mother and is joined to his wife, and the two are united into one. Now the man and his wife were both naked, but they felt no shame.' Genesis 2.21-25 NLT

Sex is for mutual pleasure and enjoyment. Our bodies are designed to experience desire, arousal, orgasm, and pleasure. Our brains are created to release hormones during sexual activity, causing us to feel good, and to feel bonded, on a brain level, with our partner. Our bodies and brains have been created so we can enjoy the act of sex!

> 'For this reason a man is to leave his father and his mother and lovingly hold to his wife, since the two have become joined as one flesh. Marriage is the beautiful design of the Almighty, a great and sacred mystery—meant to be a vivid example of Christ and his church. So every married man should be gracious to his wife just as he is gracious to himself. And every wife should be tenderly devoted to her husband.'
> Ephesians 5.31-33 TPT

God's design for sex involves intimacy; they are designed to go hand in hand. Sex with intimacy makes you relationally whole, complete, and fulfilled. Yet, our culture has fed us an alternative message: 'Sex is *just sex*; it's an act we do because we have needs. And *intimacy*? Well, that's just optional! That's something that can go on the side, only if you want it, but it's not the main meal.' Our hook-up culture, combined with the easy accessibility to pornography, communicates to people that sex is just a physical act, something that is purely for my own self-gratification—whenever I want it, and however I want it. Under that paradigm, sex is about performance, technique and orgasms.

Nothing could be further from the truth. The reality is, that sex without intimacy can leave you broken, empty, incomplete and unfulfilled.

> 'Now the man Adam knew Eve as his wife, and she conceived and gave birth to Cain, and she said, "I have obtained a man (baby boy, son) with the help of the Lord."' Genesis 4.1 AMP

> 'Adam knew [Eve as] his wife again; and she gave birth to a son and named him Seth.' Genesis 4.25 AMP

Adam *knew* his wife. He didn't just have sex with her—he knew her intimately. You see, sexuality is about being known, deeply known, just like intimacy is about being deeply known. Our sexuality involves the four elements of intimacy—belonging, being known, being affirmed and being accepted. When you belong to someone and are known, affirmed and accepted by someone sexually, you experience intimacy. In that person, you have a place of safety; you are seen, you are validated, and *you are enough*.

To experience intimacy with sex requires something of you. It involves showing up for your partner and being present, mind, body and heart, with them. It's the revealing of more of you to them. It is only as the walls go down, the layers are peeled back and you find yourselves 'in this together' in a beautiful place of vulnerability, that you allow yourself to be comforted, cherished and cared for by the closest person to you.

That's why God created sexual intimacy to be inside a marriage. Two people deeply and personally committed to each other for life, creates a safe and secure place for this level of intimacy and vulnerability to be appreciated, cherished and protected. Marriage is where you can give yourself entirely and selflessly to the care of the other person, sharing every part of you with them.

Sex is a Gift

> 'Husbands, go all out in your love for your wives, exactly as Christ did for the church—a love marked by giving, not getting. Christ's love makes the church whole. His words evoke her beauty. Everything he does and says is designed to bring the best out of her, dressing her in dazzling white silk, radiant with holiness. And that is how husbands ought to love their wives. They're really doing themselves a favor— since they're already "one" in marriage.'
> Ephesians 5.25-28 MSG

Here, Paul is redefining what a husband's leadership in marriage looks like . . . self-sacrificing love. He leads his wife by loving her for her own benefit, by cherishing her and bringing out the best in her. He leads her by serving her. His focus towards her is giving, not trying to get his own way or gain his own advantage. The husband gives himself to his wife as a gift. And she responds by giving herself to him.

> 'Wives, understand and support your husbands in ways that show your support for Christ. The husband provides leadership to his wife the way Christ does to his church, not by domineering but by cherishing. So just as the church submits to Christ as he exercises such leadership, wives should likewise submit to their husbands.'
> Ephesians 5.22-24 MSG

Sex is a gift that each partner gives the other. The gift you give, though, is not just intercourse or orgasm. The gift is you, your whole self, the most intimate part of you, baring all, hiding nothing. The gift is you loving your spouse in a way no one else can. Sex is a valuable part of that gift, something precious that should be guarded, protected and appreciated. It should never be demanded, taken from someone, controlled, used against another's will, or used to manipulate. What makes sex so beautiful, is that it is freely given.

God created and designed sex for marriage, a gift that enables a man and woman to celebrate their love through mutual pleasure and enjoyment. It was never designed to be a shameful thing! That's why pleasure is such a valuable part of sex—it is a gift you give to your spouse, and a gift you receive from your spouse. To let someone else see your personal pleasure is an extremely vulnerable act. You are allowing your pleasure to be unwrapped and seen in the invited presence of your spouse! When you get the privilege and honour of seeing your spouse's pleasure, cherish it! It's a beautiful and precious thing. Sex is a gift!

Sex is Sacrificial and Other-Centred

> *'The marriage bed must be a place of mutuality—the husband seeking to satisfy his wife, the wife seeking to satisfy her husband. Marriage is not a place to "stand up for your rights." Marriage is a decision to serve the other, whether in bed or out.'* 1 Corinthians 7.2-6 MSG

Sacrificial, other-centred sex is about serving one another. When each partner's priority is caring for and meeting their spouse's needs, sex can be mutually satisfying. It contrasts vividly with our culture and society, which says, 'sex is all about me and my needs. Sex is about my pleasure, my release; in fact, sex is *my right.*'

When sex is sacrificial, you engage in sexual intimacy with a willingness to give, even if you don't feel like receiving. When sex is other-centred, both of you are willing to go out of your way to meet each other's needs. That way, everybody wins! Sex is not designed to be one-sided, with one person giving and the other receiving. This turns sex into a power struggle between partners. Other-centred sex, on the other hand, is a place of mutuality.

Our culture and society have conveyed the message that everyone is always having sex, that everyone always wants sex, and that no one ever says 'no' to sex! But let's take a reality check. Married couples *are not* having sex all day, every day—although I'm sure some married people wish they were! But people live full, busy lives. They are tired! There will be times in your marriage when one partner is receiving pleasure and the other partner is giving pleasure, and there will be times when you don't feel like sex in the same moment that your partner does. How you navigate this in your relationship, and how you personally interpret and understand this, is critical.

If your partner decides to stop having sex because they don't feel like it anymore or because they want to punish you by turning it into some sort of 'tit for tat' game, this is incredibly damaging. It will hurt your partner and your relationship. This approach makes sex about you, which essentially is selfish. That's not God's design for sex. It's a gift you give selflessly, in order to place value on your spouse. It's a way of honouring your husband or wife, in order to bring out the best in them.

Don't allow sex in your marriage to be cheapened by making it a transaction, an obligation, or a duty. Don't keep a relationship (or sex-score) card. Be willing to give more than you receive, and it's possible that both of you will experience sexual happiness. Sex in a healthy God-honouring marriage where both partners serve each other sacrificially, has the power to enhance, empower and add life to you and your relationship!

Sacrificial, other-centred sex is where you can safely and openly talk about your needs, your preferences, and what would give you greater enjoyment. It's where you can openly talk about how you can satisfy each other, even if one partner is more 'in the mood' than the other. Sacrificial love seeks out ways to make your spouse feel safe and comfortable; it goes to great effort to understand how to care for the other person. Sacrificial love learns how to love your spouse the way they want to be loved, not necessarily how you want to love them.

Sex is Vulnerable

'Adam and his wife were both naked, and they felt no shame.'
Genesis 2.25 NIV

Marriage is designed to be a relationship that is naked without shame. In the privacy of your relationship, you can share fully with your spouse what you do not completely share with anyone else—and in that sharing and revealing of yourself to your spouse, there is no shame. This is what makes your relationship unique, precious, and distinct from all your other relationships.

Sexual intimacy is the most vulnerable act you can do with someone. We are naked, unguarded, and exposed. In this beautiful 'revealing', we are trusting our vulnerability to our spouse. If vulnerability had words, it would say, 'Am I enough for you? Do you accept me? Will you still love me? Am I still wanted?' And vulnerability replies, 'Yes! I need you. I want you.'

Marriage is the safest place for two people to be vulnerable. In a covenant relationship built on trust and acceptance, intimacy can grow. This brings freedom—to be who you really are, to love and to receive love, to hide nothing and give everything. Intimacy in marriage allows us to find freedom from rejection and shame.

Imagine sharing all of yourself with someone, only to find that you are still loved and accepted. No guilt, no shame, no embarrassment, no apologising for who you are, no pretending or covering up, and no fear of being judged, or compared, or having your performance rated. This is the kind of acceptance that enables us to bring no masks, secrets or agendas to our sexual intimacy. There are no feelings of inadequacies about your body, no 'putting your clothes on and running off before he or she wakes up' experience. There is no 'booty call' when either of you are feeling 'in the mood.' There is no wondering who else your partner has slept with this week.

Imagine sharing yourself with someone that is committed to being there for you, the next day, and the next day and the next day *for all your days*. Imagine being seen for who you really are and knowing that you are enough. Total trust. Total vulnerability. No fear. No shame. *This* is intimacy and *this* is the type of sexual relationship we have been designed to have.

Sex Builds Intimacy

> *'I know my lover is mine and I have everything in you, for we delight ourselves in each other.'* Song of Songs 2.16 TPT

The goal of sex is intimacy, and intimacy enhances your relationship. When you are intimate with someone, you feel connected to them, you feel close to them, you are completely known by them. Intimacy can only be experienced through relationship.

Sex bonds you together. Sex draws a man and a woman together in a close, attached, intimate way. When two people are sexually intimate, a bonding hormone (oxytocin, the same hormone that is released during breastfeeding enabling a mother to bond with her baby), and other hormones (vasopressin, endorphins and dopamine) are released, causing the couple to form a brain-level attachment as well as a strong emotional bond with each other. It is amazing to think that God has created your body to enjoy sex and that he designed your brain to release chemicals during sex that cause you to bond and stay unified to your partner.

Oxytocin is one of the hormones that makes you feel connected to your partner. Every time you experience an orgasm, oxytocin (often called the 'cuddle hormone') floods your brain, reducing the effects of stress. Vasopressin is the hormone that induces feelings of trust, leading you to recognize your mate as special; dopamine is the 'feel-good' hormone which creates a sense of euphoria, while endorphins have a sedative effect. This is why when you make love, you can feel closer to your partner, and the closer you feel, the more you want to make love. These hormones work together to create that special feeling of deep trust and commitment between couples.

Sex unifies us—but a regular sex life also requires you to stay united in your relationship. That means you need to address anything that has the potential to divide you or pull you apart. If there is any wedge of bitterness, anger, resentment, unforgiveness or pride between you, deal with it quickly, and forgive, so that you can stay unified. In fact, one of the roles of sexuality is 'to bond and energize the couple as they go through good and bad times.'[2]

Sex brings healing. When a couple come up against each other in a disagreement and can see no way to resolve it, sex can connect them together! Sexual intimacy releases the relational tension; after sex, a couple will discover that their walls have dropped, they feel softer towards each other, and they are able to repair and resolve their differences.

---

[2] B McCarthy, Sex made simple: clinical strategies for sexual issues in therapy, PESI Publishing & Media, 2015, p 129.

Great sex is a by-product of a healthy marriage. If you are going to enjoy satisfying sexual intimacy, you need to build a healthy marriage! A healthy marriage meets the need for intimacy and security better than any other relationship. A healthy marriage promotes individual growth and maturity.

Your Spouse can not Complete You

Your spouse can not satisfy your every emotional, intellectual, spiritual, physical, recreational and sexual need. They cannot live up to your every fantasy or meet every sexual desire whenever you need it. These are unrealistic expectations. Ask yourself, does every one of your sexual desires *need* to be met? Why? Why not? Marriage is not your guarantee of having sex whenever you feel like it!

The truth is, sex is great, it is momentarily satisfying, and it does enhance your marriage, but *it cannot make your life complete*. We live in a world that idolises sex, but sex was never designed to fulfil us. Our fulfillment, our sufficiency, and our completeness come from knowing Jesus Christ. Jesus alone satisfies our every need, quenches our every thirst, lasts forever, and never disappoints.

- Discussion Questions for Couples -

What do you believe God desires for our sex life within our marriage?

Do you see sex as a good gift from God for you to enjoy?

What do you think the purpose of sex is?

How important is sex in our marriage to you? Why?

What parts of you would you like to share more with me?

How can we build the different forms of intimacy (spiritual, recreational, intellectual, physical, emotional & sexual) into our marriage?

2.
THE POWER OF SEX

Understanding your brain, body
and sexual desire

God only makes good things. He created your body and He called it good. God does not make mistakes and He does not make rubbish. God creates with purpose. Every part of your body is good, including your genitals.

> *'So God created mankind in his own image, in the image of God he created them; male and female he created them. God blessed them and said to them, "Be fruitful and increase in number."' Genesis 1.27-28 NIV*

> *'God saw all that he had made, and it was very good.' Genesis 1.31 NIV*

The male and female genitals are beautifully handcrafted, designed by God to fit perfectly together. He put an incredible amount of detail into these wonderful creations, placing numerous nerve endings in the genital region. This intricate planning was so we would find the experience of coming together to make love fun and enjoyable. God wanted our sexual experience to be pleasurable!

SEXUAL ANATOMY

Although God put so much detail and care into His design for our beautiful genitals, he created them, first and foremost, to be private. They're tucked away, protected and easily covered. Our genitals are not for everyone to see, touch and enjoy. That's why we wear underwear and cover up in public. But in marriage, we have the special privilege of sharing our genitals with each other!

> *'That is why a man leaves his father and mother and is united to his wife, and they become one flesh. Adam and his wife were both naked, and they felt no shame.' Genesis 2.24-25 NIV*

Adam and Eve were free to share any and every part of themselves with each other. This is God's perfect plan—that we would unashamedly share every part of our body with our spouse.

It is not uncommon, however, for people to have a negative association with their genitals. You may have even cringed when I referred to genitals as, 'beautiful creations.' There can be various reasons why we are uncomfortable about this—some simply find it embarrassing or awkward; for others, it evokes a sense of shame or guilt; and some people cringe because it brings up difficult memories of trauma or abuse.

Whatever the reason, when we have a negative association with our genitals, it impacts our sexual intimacy in marriage. As hard as it may be to challenge or face our discomfort, there is an alternative way of thinking about your genitals!

> **Pause and reflect:**
>
> *Growing up, how did your parents refer to genitals?*

When I was twenty-eight years old, I became pregnant with my first child. I was a few months off completing a Masters of Sexual Health when I found myself in my Obstetrician's office for my routine pregnancy check-up. As it was my first pregnancy, I had no idea what to expect. Sitting across from my doctor, I attempted to discuss some symptoms I was experiencing, hoping he might reassure me that everything was as it should be. I wanted to know if there was anything I should worry about, and what was 'normal.'

As I described what I was experiencing, I noticed myself referring to my vagina as 'down there.' I was baffled! I could not believe how uncomfortable I was! Here I was, about to graduate with a degree in Sexual Health, having studied sexual anatomy and human sexual behaviour for the past few years, and on the other side of the desk was a doctor with decades of experience birthing babies, a man who saw women's vaginas all day, every day—and yet, I found it so uncomfortable to even say the word in front of him!

One of the reasons I was uncomfortable saying the names of genitals was because they were not openly spoken about during my growing-up years. This is a common theme for many people. Some of us grew up never hearing our parents give our genitals their correct anatomical term—penis, vagina, or vulva.

Perhaps you were taught to call your genitals a pet name? For the penis, this may have been a name like, 'dinky,' 'monkey,' 'wee-wee,' 'weaner,' 'pee-pee,' 'doodle' or 'willy.' Pet names that parents have commonly used for the vagina are 'front bum,' 'fanny,' 'cookie,' 'muffin,' 'ginny,' 'girl bits' and 'foo-foo.' For others of us, any reference to the genitals was avoided. It was almost like we pretended they weren't there or that they weren't even a body part.

How crazy that we should not be able to talk comfortably about a body part that every human has! Why is it that we can call an elbow, an elbow, and a nose, a nose, but we are unable to use the words *penis* or *vagina* with our kids? No wonder we have so much shame and embarrassment attached to the genitals! By not normalising it, we have implied that we can't talk about it, and that this is a shameful part of our body.

If you are already a parent, you can empower your children by teaching them the proper names! In fact, one of the most helpful ways to equip children to disclose sexual abuse, is to teach them the correct terminology for genitalia.[1] We need to push past the awkwardness and empower our children to use the correct names.

From the Womb

Males and females start their life in the womb looking similar. The baby's sex is set at conception. From conception until the sixth week of pregnancy, every baby's genitals look the same—whether the baby is male or female.

Sex development begins in the seventh week of pregnancy. The testes in male embryos secrete testosterone, kicking off the development of male genitalia—a penis and scrotum. For female embryos, in the absence of testosterone, female genitalia develop—a clitoris and labia. The penis for a male is the clitoris for the female. The scrotum for a male is the labia for the female.

The penis and the clitoris develop from the same origin. The penis grows outside the body, while the clitoris grows inside the body. Both organs have a glans, a foreskin and a shaft containing two cylinders of erectile tissue that fill with blood and engorge during sexual arousal. During orgasm, both male and female pelvic muscles contract at the same intervals of eight-tenths of a second.

The labia and the scrotum also develop from the same foetal tissue. Both of these organs have soft elastic skin and, after puberty, are covered with pubic hair. The scrotum is the fusion of the two folds, and has a seam down the middle where it would have separated to form a labia if it had instead developed into female genitals.

---

[1] S.K. Wurtele and M.C. Kenny, 'Partnering with parents to prevent childhood sexual abuse', Child Abuse Review, vol 19. no. 2, 2010, pp130-152.

Female Sexual Anatomy

Let's take a moment to explore the female external genitalia. Many of us use the word 'vagina' in reference to a female's genitals, but this is technically incorrect. The vagina is only one part of the female genitalia. The correct reference for the female external genitalia is the vulva.

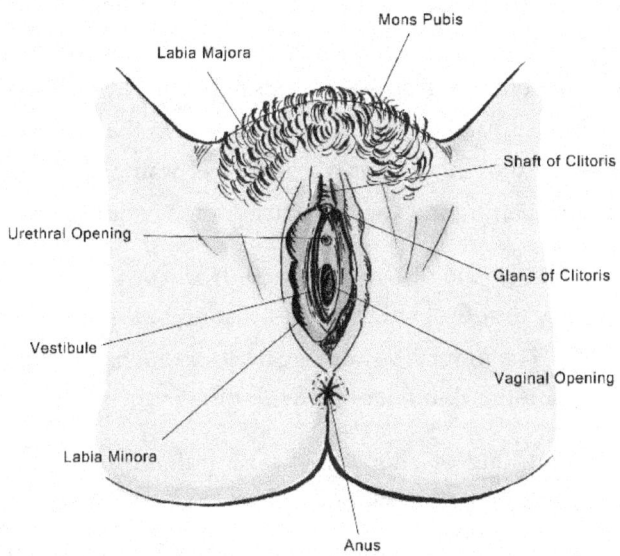

Female External Genitalia

THE VULVA is the external female genitalia, consisting of the mons pubis, labia majora, labia minora, clitoris, vestibule, urethra opening, and vaginal opening. The vulva plays an important role in the woman's sexual response.

Vulvas are not all neat, pink and perfect. All vulvas are unique. Vulvas come in different shapes, sizes and colours—there are no two vulvas the same, just as there are no two identical penises.

THE MONS PUBIS (also known as mons veneris) is the fleshly mound above the clitoris. This extends over the pubic bone, is covered in pubic hair, and is rich in nerve endings. Both sexes have a mons pubis, however it is more prominent in females.

THE LABIA MINORA & LABIA MAJORA are the inner (labia minora) and outer (labia majora) lips that begin at the clitoris and extend to the opening of the vagina. The labia minora covers and protects the vaginal and urethra openings. They are smooth and hairless, rich in blood vessels and nerve endings, and have sweat glands. The inner lips are more sensitive to touch than the outer lips. When aroused, the inner lips darken, becoming engorged and elongated, and opening the vaginal entrance for penetration.

The labia majora are the outer lips. These two thick folds of skin are made up of fatty tissue, covered with sweat and oil-secreting glands, and pubic hair. The outer lips are sensitive to touch, and the erectile tissue underneath the skin engorges with blood when aroused.

The labia can be long or short, thick and bulging or thin and flat, smooth or wrinkly, and they are often asymmetrical, meaning that one lip is usually longer than the other. For some women, their labia minora can be larger than their labia majora, while for other women it is the other way around. The labia vary in colour from pink to purple to dark brown and this can change as the woman gets older. Vulvar swelling is a more reliable indicator of arousal than lubrication.

THE VAGINA is not 'everything down there.' It is the internal reproductive canal that leads to the uterus. The vagina is a collapsed, muscular tube which is closed at the inner end and slopes backwards from the vaginal opening to the tailbone. The vagina connects the vulva and external female genitalia with the internal female reproductive organs (cervix, ovaries, fallopian tubes, and uterus).

In an unaroused state the vagina is, on average, about 9–11cm long, and the vaginal walls are touching. These walls are soft, elastic, thick and flexible—somewhat similar to the lining inside your cheeks. The vaginal walls can be spread wide enough to birth a baby; they also can enlarge and extend during sexual arousal to contain the penis during intercourse.

The outer third of the vagina is engorged with erectile tissue which swells at the vaginal opening making the penis fit snuggly. This is the most sensitive part of the vagina; the inner two thirds of the vagina have fewer nerve endings and are therefore less sensitive.

During sexual arousal, drops of fluid are secreted from the engorged blood vessels in the vagina. This inbuilt lubrication allows intercourse to be pleasurable and comfortable. Lubrication is a significant (but not the only) part of the arousal process.

THE CLITORIS has a glans, foreskin and shaft. It is the only organ in the human body with the sole function of bringing sexual pleasure, and it is the most sensitive structure in the female body. The clitoris is shaped like wishbone, having two 'legs' within the tissue of the vulva that extend all the way to the vaginal opening. Most of the clitoris is hidden inside the pelvic area.

The *glans clitoris* (clitoral glans) is a smooth, round lump of tissue above the urethra opening. It ranges in size and is protected by the *clitoral hood* (foreskin) which is attached to the labia minora. To see your clitoral glans, gently separate the labia minora and pull back the hood. The clitoris has more than eight thousand nerve endings, all packed into a much smaller shaft than a penis, making it very sensitive to touch.

The *clitoral shaft* contains two cylinders of spongy erectile tissue that become engorged and erect when a woman is aroused. When the clitoris is engorged with blood, it retracts and hides under its hood to protect its sensitive tip. It is not easily accessible; the clitoral hood must be purposefully pulled back in order to touch and stimulate it. Some women may find direct stimulation of the clitoris pleasurable; others find it too sensitive or painful. Every woman is different.

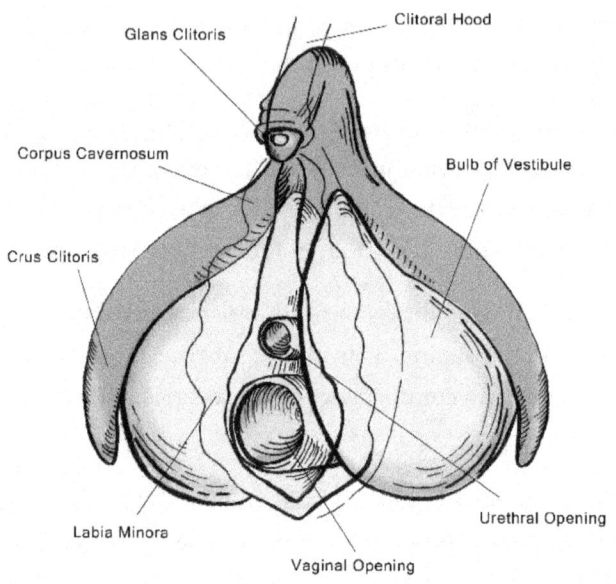

Anatomy of the clitoris

THE PERINEUM refers to the skin beneath the vaginal opening and above the anus. Under the perineum are blood vessels and erectile tissue that swell during arousal. It is rich in nerve endings and therefore extremely sensitive. Gently touching the perineum area can be highly arousing.

THE G-SPOT is a sensitive area on the front upper wall of the vagina, beneath the urethra. This spongy erectile tissue encircles the urethra and fills with blood during arousal. When a woman is aroused, deep massage with two fingers, or deep pressure from the penis during intercourse (rear-entry or woman-on-top positions), applied to the G-spot, can be highly pleasurable. A G-spot orgasm is a clitoral orgasm.

Male Sexual Anatomy

The male sexual anatomy, located outside of the body, includes the penis, scrotum, and testicles.

THE PENIS has four functions: urination, pleasure, penetration and ejaculation. The average penis length is 8-9.5cm in the flaccid state and the average erect penis length ranges from 12–15cm. The penis has three parts — the root, which extends into the pelvis and is attached to the pelvic bones; the shaft, which is the body of the penis; and the glans.

The penis contains three cylinders of spongy tissue which swell with blood during sexual arousal, causing the penis to become larger, longer and more rigid, creating an erection. The urethra runs through the middle cylinder and ends in the glans penis.

Ejaculate and urine are released through the urethra. The bladder is closed off when a male is sexually aroused, minimising the chance of semen and urine mixing. The penis is able to enlarge within moments, becoming firm and changing from a tube that passes urine to one that releases semen. The function of the penis is erectile and ejaculatory; erectile function is related to the health of the male's cardiovascular system, and ejaculation involves the vas deferens, prostate gland, seminal vesicles and muscle contractions.

An erection is a natural function of the body that can happen in the conscious and unconscious state. Men have erections as they sleep, generally during REM (rapid eye movement) sleep periods. Experiencing night or morning erections are healthy signs that the nerve and blood supply to the penis function well. For men in good health, this can continue as they age.

Automatic or spontaneous erections are common in younger men, however, as a man gets older, he may require direct stimulation of the penis to achieve an erection. This is normal and natural and an opportunity to enhance pleasure and sensation.

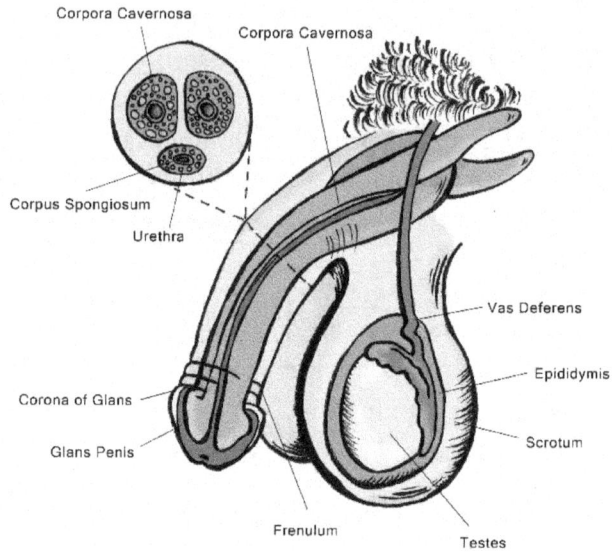

Male Genitalia

THE GLANS PENIS is known as 'the head.' It has a high concentration of nerve endings, is smooth and hairless and is the most sensitive part of the penis. The ridge that separates the glans from the shaft is the most sensitive part of the glans. The glans is covered with a layer of skin called 'foreskin' which is removed if the male is circumcised. At the tip of the penis is the urethra opening, called the *meatus*, the tube that transports urine and semen.

THE SHAFT is the body of the penis and loosely hangs when unaroused. When a male is sexually excited, blood expands the penis, resulting in an erection. The skin of the penis is hairless.

THE FRENULUM is the ridge of skin on the underside of the glans penis that meets the shaft. It can be highly sensitive and sexually arousing.

THE SCROTUM is a sac of soft, wrinkled skin that is covered with hair, and houses the testes. It is not uncommon for one testicle to hang lower than the other. The scrotum is flexible and can relax and dangle freely in warm weather, and contract in cold weather, drawing the testes closer to the body.

THE TESTES have an important job. They produce and store sperm and supply the male sex hormone, testosterone. Testosterone influences sexual desire and male physical characteristics. The epididymis, a long tube attached to the testes, lives inside the scrotum and carries sperm from the testes to the vas deferens. The vas deferens stores and transports sperm. Sperm have quite a journey to make from the testes to the epididymis to the vas deferens and finally out through the urethra. It's a long-distance swim for these little sperm!

THE PERINEUM extends from between the scrotum to the anus. Gentle massage of the perineum can bring sexual pleasure.

To enjoy a healthy sex life in your marriage, you need to have a positive association with your body and your genitals. You can love your genitals! This is different to glorifying the penis and vagina, and it is different to making it 'all about what your genitals want,' as if they have a mind of their own. Instead, it is about a healthy appreciation of what God has created, with no shame or embarrassment. It involves understanding God's plan and purpose for the genitals, and why he called them, 'good.'

SEXUAL RESPONSE CYCLE

Sexual functioning is how the body moves through the sexual response cycle of desire, arousal and orgasm with ease and satisfaction. Physiological changes and responses occur as a person is sexually aroused. In their book 'Human Sexual Response,'[2] Masters and Johnson articulated a four-phase model of human sexual response: Excitement, Plateau, Orgasm and Resolution.

In any sexual encounter, a person may experience some or all of these phases, usually with different timing. The intensity of each sexual response can vary for lovers, and it is common for partners to reach orgasm at different times. Learning how your body responds in each phase of the sexual response cycle and discovering how it differs from your partner's response can be empowering. This insight will give you a deeper understanding of how your bodies respond to arousal and how to enhance your sexual experience and couple satisfaction. It is helpful to understand the four phases of sexual response:

1. Excitement

This phase is the initial building of sexual arousal. It occurs when stimulation begins and can last from a few minutes to several hours. During this phase, muscle tension increases, heart rate and blood pressure increase, and breathing is accelerated. Skin may become flushed, with red blotches appearing on the chest and back, the breasts swell, and nipples become erect.

The woman's breasts become fuller during the excitement phase; stimulation of the nipples encourages the release of the hormone oxytocin, which in turn creates a pleasurable sensation in the genitals as the clitoral head emerges from its hood, the labia minora

---

[2] W.H. Masters & V.E. Johnson, Human Sexual Response, Bantam Books, 1966

(inner lips) and the vaginal walls begin to swell with blood, and blood vessels force fluid through the vaginal walls, creating a lubricated environment.

For the male, blood flows to the penis, creating an erection, causing the penis to enlarge and rise to an angle. His testicles enlarge, his scrotum contracts, and a lubricating fluid called pre-ejaculate begins secreting. Pre-ejaculate is clear and colourless and is released from the male urethra prior to ejaculation. Pre-ejaculate fluid has the possibility of containing sperm.

2. Plateau

The 'plateau phase' is when levels of sexual arousal intensify, flooding your body with pleasure. As a result, breathing, heart rate and blood pressure increase, muscle tension builds, and muscle spasms or contractions may begin in the feet, face, buttocks and hands.

The woman's vagina continues to swell during this phase, with the inner labia doubling in size and changing colour to a dark purple. The woman's clitoris also becomes highly sensitive and retracts to avoid direct stimulation from the penis. The clitoral body stiffens and extends. Her breasts continue to swell, the nipples retract into the breasts and the vagina opens wide and deep inside.

The man's penis is fully erect at this point; his testicles increase in size and withdraw up into the scrotum. If arousal does not continue to ejaculation, the swollen testicles become uncomfortable. This feeling of fullness is popularly referred to as 'blue balls' but is temporary and does not cause harm. In the 'plateau' phase, the male learns to control the timing of his sexual response and the women learns to trust her body to let go and be free in the moment.

Lubrication is a significant part of the female sexual arousal process; however it is not the key indicator that the woman is adequately aroused for penetration. A woman's readiness for sexual intercourse comes when she has been stimulated until her body is fully aroused — the signs of this are: increased heart rate, faster breathing, muscle tension, and genital swelling, combined with lubrication. Adequate stimulation takes time but is essential for a woman's comfort during intercourse. Lubrication can also be impacted by physiological factors such as estrogen levels (particularly if the woman is breastfeeding), stress and diet. The key to pleasure is to take things slowly, spend extra time on sexual stimulation and use lubricant to assist in arousal.

3. Orgasm

Orgasm is the release of muscular tension through a series of quick, rhythmic contractions of the pelvic floor muscles. This marks the climax of the sexual response cycle, is the shortest of the phases and generally lasts only a few seconds. General characteristics of this phase include involuntary muscle tightening and contractions, pelvic thrusts, high blood pressure and heart rate, and deep breathing, along with a sudden, forceful release of sexual tension.

In women, the muscles of the vagina, urethra and anus contract. The uterus experiences rhythmic contractions from the flood of oxytocin which brings waves of pleasure to the woman, followed by a feeling of physical satisfaction and calm.

In men, the rhythmic contractions of the muscles are felt in the pelvic area, near the anus, the base of the penis, and the head of the penis. These contractions propel semen through the urethra and out of the head of the penis, resulting in the ejaculation of semen. Male orgasm and ejaculation occur simultaneously but are different. Orgasm refers to the muscular contractions that release sexual tension, and ejaculation is the release of semen.

4. Resolution

In the 'resolution' phase, the body gradually moves back to its normal unaroused state and functioning, and swollen and erect body parts relax and return to their original size and colour. This phase gives people a wonderful sex 'afterglow'; the brain releases 'feel-good' chemicals called endorphins, making us feel relaxed, content and fatigued. We can feel closer and more intimate with our partner.

With continued sexual stimulation, some women can return to the 'orgasm' phase and may experience additional orgasms. This is because their genitals take longer to return to their unaroused normal state than men.

For men, blood flows out of the penis during this phase, their erections gradually subside, the scrotum descends, and the testes decrease in size. Men are unable to experience multiple orgasms in a short space of time. After orgasm and ejaculation, they require a refractory period. This is the man's 'recovery time,' an interval where the body is too sensitive to respond to further sexual stimulation and erection, and orgasm is unlikely.

The length of the refractory period differs among men and lengthens with age. Young men may need only minutes to 'recover,' while older men may need anything from a few hours to a few days. It is common for males to experience muscle aches in the back or thighs even the following day.

Because of these differences, women seek connection after sex, while men tend to be quickly fatigued and want to sleep. Don't take this personally. These are biological differences but can be easily resolved.

By going to sleep in each other's arms or taking a moment to be affectionate with each other before falling asleep, both partners win!

Even though females and males have a biological sexual response cycle, every person is unique. How the sexual experience plays out, the length and duration of the sexual cycle, and the satisfaction it brings, will depend on the health of the relationship, including the level of safety, agreement, intimacy and communication between the two people involved.

DESIRE

The purpose of sexual desire is to direct us into connection with another person. Desire is more than a need for pleasure—it is a need for intimacy. Sexual desire drives us to be deeply and relationally known by another. It is defined as the urge, craving or want for sex. It is driven by the sex hormone testosterone and involves the presence of sexual thoughts, dreams, and fantasies. In fact, many people now include 'desire' as a vital first stage in the sexual response cycle, effectively turning the original model into a five-phase sexual response model; desire, excitement (arousal), plateau, orgasm and satisfaction (resolution).[3]

We often think that sexual desire 'just appears,' that you only need to see your spouse naked or dressed up in a suit to get the thought, 'I'd like to have sex!' Or, you have a sexual dream about your spouse and wake up thinking, 'I feel like sex!' This is often referred to as 'spontaneous desire.'

Men and women experience spontaneous sexual desire, but it occurs more often in men than in women. Spontaneous desire for women can be related to a particular time in her menstrual cycle, at the start of a

---

[3] H.S. Kaplan, Disorders of Sexual Desire, Simon & Schuster, New York, 1979.

new relationship where romance and passionate energy leads to effortless sexual response, or when you are separated from your spouse for a period of time, where the resulting hunger or need to be sexually together again may fuel spontaneous desire.[4]

While the sexual response models are especially useful for understanding male sexual response, they are less relevant to our understanding of the female sexual response. *Hello, Rosemary Basson*! In her research, Basson found that women in long-term, committed relationships are often consumed with the busyness of life, tend to be more fatigued and distracted, and therefore experience more 'responsive desire' than 'spontaneous desire.'[5]

Responsive desire is just as normal and natural as spontaneous desire. Basson's model suggests a woman's motivation to engage in sexual intimacy may come more from her need for intimacy in the relationship than her need for physical sexual arousal or her need to release sexual tension.

Jenny has been married to Mark for twelve years. As a mum of four boys, she lives a hectic life and is constantly 'hustling.' She loves her husband and enjoys her sex life, but if she were honest, she rarely has sex on her mind. Her husband is attentive and caring, and Jenny experiences trust, respect and affection from him. As a couple, they share open and intimate communication. Jenny feels safe to be vulnerable with Mark. She enjoys intimacy when they are together and feels pleasure from Mark's sensual touch. Even when Jenny does not experience orgasm (although of course, that would be nice!) she does experience sexual satisfaction. This is because her motivation for sex is not solely to experience an orgasm. Her motivation

---

[4] A Harding, Rosemary Basson: working to normalise women's sexual reality, The Lancet, Elsevier, Volume 369, Issue 9559, 3 February 2007, pp 363

[5] R Basson, The Female Sexual Response: A Different Model, Journal of Sex & Marital Therapy, vol. 26 no.1, 2000, pp 51-65.

includes all 'the wonderful feels' she gets from Mark as he makes her feel emotionally and physically close, intimate, bonded and connected. For Jenny, sex is much more than just the act of intercourse.

A women's sexual response can start in a neutral place. From this place of neutrality, she notices the potential for a sexual occasion, her partner may desire her, or she sees the relational value of being sexually intimate. It could be emotional connection and bonding, sharing vulnerability or expressing love and affection—and so, she engages in romantic touch and sexual stimulation with her spouse.

As she receives gentle and relaxing sensual touch, or another form of romance and intimacy by her partner, her body starts to get aroused. As her body becomes aroused, the vagina swells and lubricates, her brain chemistry changes, and her desire for sex kicks in. In turn, that desire for sex increases her body's want for further sexual arousal.

Relaxation, along with giving herself permission to experience and enjoy sexual touch, can arouse and awaken her body and brain to the point of sexual responsiveness and pleasure. This is 'responsive sexual desire.' From a place of being 'sexually neutral,' women are able to be sexually aroused before they even desire sex. *Sexual arousal stimulates the woman's desire for sex.*

Desire Differences

Think of it like this: My husband and I are different in many things. He loves to sleep and could sleep anytime, anywhere. I am the opposite, once I'm awake in the morning, I am up and ready for the day. We rarely exercise at the same time. He might be motivated to go for a run when I want to relax. We crave different dinner cuisines and have different movie preferences. Couples don't always feel like the same thing at the same time.

It is normal for two people to have different levels of desire. The literature on sex differences suggests that in general, women are less interested in sex than men. However, this is not always the case, as in some relationships, the woman has the higher sex drive. Sexual desire discrepancies in a marriage are normal. If you and your spouse want different frequencies of sexual activity or desire sex at different times, this can be navigated through communication and compromise.

Have you ever wondered why you don't want sex all the time? If you find yourself not wanting to have sex at every opportunity you get, or preferring to share a chocolate dessert or watch a movie with your spouse over having sex, that's normal. There is nothing wrong with that, despite what society often leads us to believe.

Accelerator and Brakes

What turns you on? And what turns you off? The things that bring on desire or turn it off are unique for each of us. Sexual response researchers, Bancroft and Janssen, describe desire as having an accelerator pedal and a brake pedal.[6] There are many things that can effectively 'put the brakes on'—things like fear of criticism, unresolved conflict, stress at work, too many distractions, medications or just the wrong type of touch (or the right touch too soon!). Learn what turns your spouse on and what turns him or her off. Remember too, that building desire requires 'revving up your engine' and taking your foot off your own brake pedal! This is explored further in Emily Nagoski's book 'Come as you are'.[7]

---

[6] E Janssen & J Bancroft, The dual control model: the role of sexual inhibition & excitation in sexual arousal and behavior, The Kinsey Institute Series, 2006.

[7] E Nagoski, Come as You Are: The Surprising New Science that will transform your sex life, Simon & Schuster, 2015

HOW TO BUILD YOUR SEXUAL DESIRE

Consider for a moment. What builds your sexual desire? What can your spouse do to help build your desire? Here are a few key factors in building sexual desire:

Build it in your Mind

Desire can be cultivated. Use your imagination. The book of 'Song of Songs,' is an account of two lovers who express their longing for each other with imagination, creativity, and romance.

If you don't think much about sex, be intentional about growing and developing your sexual thoughts. Even if you only have one sexual thought a week, instead of making it a fleeting thought that you dismiss, push away or ignore, sit with it awhile. Recognise and acknowledge that you are having a sexual thought and activate your imagination about how you could be sexual with your spouse. How could you greet your spouse? What could you be wearing? What could you say to him or her? How might your spouse respond to your kiss? What might you do next? Would you dance together, rip their clothes off . . . or tease them?!

By engaging your mind with creativity and imagination, you can build on the sexual thoughts you have. Building desire in your mind grows your anticipation for your spouse, and anticipation is a powerful way of building sexual desire. There is nothing wrong with fantasising sexually about you and your spouse.

Be Present in the Moment

Being present in anything can be a challenge when our mind is distracted, and sex is no exception. Women are great multitaskers! Even during sex, we can be thinking about the laundry, what we will cook for dinner tomorrow night, if the kids' uniforms need washing, all while wondering 'when is this going to finish?!' We can also be caught up with focusing on our partner's enjoyment, wondering, 'am I doing this right?', 'is he enjoying this?'—or for men, wondering 'will I stay hard long enough?' or 'will I come too soon?'

Worry, fear and distraction can kill desire and cause us to be more like a spectator than a participant during sex. It is far more fun, however, to be 'on the field,' and 'in the game,' than to simply be a spectator of pleasure. So, show up in the sexual experience! Be present and engage yourself. Shut out any unhelpful thoughts and replace them with focussed, helpful thoughts. One beautiful way of being present with your partner during sex is to open your eyes and look at each other.

Have an Open Mind

Always keep desire on the table. You can do this by simply staying open to the possibility of having sex. You may not feel any desire when you begin engaging in sexual intimacy—but if you choose to intentionally relax your body, let go of the cares of the world, tune in to your senses, respond to touch, engage your mind with positive affirming thoughts about you and your spouse, and focus on what is enjoyable and pleasurable, you may be surprised to find that your desire for sex soon follows! Next time you don't feel like it, just do it anyway! Ask your spouse to help bring you along until you are 'in the mood,' and see if you end up enjoying it.

Build Anticipation and Passion

You can keep the flame alive and cultivate desire by building anticipation and passion. Create an atmosphere for pleasure by listening, inviting, teasing, kissing, tempting, complimenting, romancing, and seducing. Think back on what you did together when you were dating. Did you write love letters to each other? Did you buy cute little cards or chocolates just to make your partner feel special? Did you plan special dates or surprises? What did you say or do to make each other feel special? This romance, love and affection does not need to stop when you are married, so don't be lazy! Keep cultivating it in your marriage!

Own It

You need to own and cultivate your sexual desire. You need to give yourself permission to be a sexual being, to allow yourself to feel what desire, arousal and orgasm can bring, and to enjoy intimacy and closeness for yourself. Your spouse can put all the effort they can into helping you enjoy sex, but in the end, you still need to 'own your sexuality.' He or she can romance you, give affection, compliment you, be a team in housework, and try different ways of touching you, but you still need to let go of any resistance, and allow desire to grow.

However, there are things that you and your spouse can do together to enhance your desire for sexual intimacy, including educating yourself! Start by reading some credible sex-education books together or individually and talk about what you are learning.

SEXUAL DYSFUNCTIONS

We can all experience sexual problems from time to time. Men can have difficulty obtaining an erection, or ejaculate more quickly than they would like. Women can have difficulty becoming lubricated or reaching orgasm. The occasional sexual problem is normal. You are not a robot or a machine.

Sexual dysfunctions, on the other hand, are problems that persist, causing significant personal and relational distress. People with sexual dysfunctions often avoid sexual intimacy due to a sense of inadequacy, incompetence, shame, anxiety, or even a fear of 'failure.' It is important to realise that ultimatums around sexual dysfunction are always destructive.

There are various reasons why a person may experience sexual dysfunction. These could be physiological—medical, neurological or nerve conditions, a side effect of particular medications, hormone imbalances, fatigue, or alcohol and drug use. Sexual dysfunction can also result from psychological issues such as low self-esteem, anxiety, depression, family of origin difficulties, past abuse or trauma, performance anxiety, sexual guilt and shame. For some, dysfunctions simply reflect a lack of sexual knowledge, poor understanding of genital anatomy and normal sexual functioning, ineffective or inadequate sexual stimulation from their spouse, or unhealthy attitudes or beliefs about sexual intimacy.

And lastly, sexual dysfunction can be caused by relational issues. Conflict, power and control dynamics, or unrealistic expectations by your partner, can all lead to sexual dysfunction. A person's sexual dysfunction can also be caused by their partner's sexual dysfunction. For example, a woman might experience sexual pain during intercourse. Her partner then worries that he could cause her pain, and this in turn can make him resist having an erection, creating erectile dysfunction.

Sexual Pain Disorder

Dyspareunia is genital pain experienced prior, during or after sexual intercourse. It can affect males and females, though usually for different reasons. Sexual pain in men is mostly associated with genital infections and irritation of the penile glans during sexual contact, whereas sexual pain in women is commonly caused by a lack of lubrication. In this case, additional foreplay or artificial lubrication can help. Female sexual pain can also be caused by vaginal infections, sexually transmitted infections (STIs), endometriosis, pelvic inflammatory disease, or structural disorders of the reproductive organs. Psychological factors such as unresolved guilt, anxiety, and a history of sexual trauma can also contribute to genital pain.

Vaginismus occurs when the pelvic muscles around the vagina involuntarily go into spasms, either preventing penetration or making it very painful. Men describe this as 'feeling like you are penetrating a brick wall.' Vaginismus can occur whether you come into marriage as a virgin or have had previous sexual experiences. It generally happens when the genital area is touched, either with a finger or when attempting intercourse. Inserting a tampon, or a gynaecological examination may even be painful. Vaginismus can be treated; in the meantime, however, if intercourse is not possible due to the discomfort, a woman can still experience sexual desire, arousal and even orgasm, even without penetration.

Sexual Arousal Disorder

Where a person's body does not respond to sexual stimulation, this can influence genital swelling, lubrication, or achieving and sustaining an erection. This is accompanied by difficulty experiencing pleasure, excitement and arousal.

Female Sexual Arousal Disorder is the ongoing difficulty in getting aroused or staying aroused and adequately lubricated during and until completion of sexual activity.

Erectile Dysfunction is the inability to achieve or sustain an erection long enough to complete the sexual act. You may occasionally lose an erection due to fatigue, stress or drinking too much alcohol. However, persistent ongoing erectile dysfunction may result from high blood pressure, high cholesterol, diabetes or heart disease and should be discussed with your medical doctor.

Some indicators of erectile dysfunction can include: rarely getting an erection, getting a firm erection but unable to sustain it before intercourse commences, or having a strong erection during masturbation or oral sex but losing the erection during intercourse. You may even avoid relational intimacy or any sexual activity with your spouse because you fear losing your erection. Erectile dysfunction is a multifaceted problem that impacts not only the body, but also the mind, emotions, self-esteem and relational intimacy.

There is a lot of pressure on a man to perform well during intercourse; to be 'successful' at having sex. The reality is, that if a man doesn't get an erection, intercourse is not possible. In some relationships, if a man loses an erection, the woman can tend to take it personally, presuming her man is not attracted to her. She may interpret the loss of erection as 'something is wrong with me,' which only adds to the man's pressure to 'perform,' and leaves a man feeling as if he has failed his wife physically, sexually and emotionally. This can be devastating.

A man can experience anxiety and therefore erectile dysfunction, because of the need to 'impress his partner.' In fact, the more anxious and concerned a man becomes about his sexual ability, the more likely he is to suffer performance anxiety. This can turn into a vicious cycle where anxiety leads to failure, and failure heightens anxiety.

Premature Ejaculation

Premature ejaculation in men is ejaculation before or shortly after penetration. It occurs with minimal stimulation, and before the person wishes it to happen. If premature ejaculation has been present for six months or more, it happens on all (or nearly all) occasions of sexual activity, and is causing the person distress, it is regarded as sexual dysfunction. A man should have enough control over his ejaculatory process to reasonably determine when he wishes to ejaculate, and to be able to adjust the timing of his release in order to take the needs of his partner into consideration.

Orgasmic Disorder

The delay or inability to reach orgasm in a woman following a normal sexual excitement phase of sufficient intensity, is called 'orgasmic disorder.' For women who are unable to orgasm at all, this is referred to as 'anorgasmia.' In men who have difficulty ejaculating during intercourse, despite being capable of ejaculating during masturbation or oral sex, this is called, 'delayed ejaculation.'

Sexual Desire Disorder

This refers to a lack of desire for sexual activity. A woman who does not experience orgasm or a man with erection difficulties, can over time, develop low sexual desire. It is understandable, of course, that an unsatisfied sex life can make you not want more of it! However, if you are experiencing low sexual desire, there may be reasons for that—medication side effects, mental health issues, life stress, or even low hormone levels. It is always recommended that you get checked by a doctor before deciding to settle for low sexual desire.

SEXUAL DYSFUNCTION IS NOT YOUR FINAL DESTINATION

Don't settle for living with a sexual dysfunction. Experiencing a sexual dysfunction can feel frustrating and isolating; it can leave you feeling like a failure or thinking you have let your spouse down. While this can be distressing, remember that it is *normal* to experience sexual dysfunction or have sexual problems at some stage in your life.

Sex isn't always perfect. However, if you are experiencing sexual dysfunction, chances are there is something deeper to discover from it. The cause could be in your mind, your body or in your relationship. I encourage you to explore all the options together.

Go Deeper

When differences arise in any part of your relationship, this is an opportunity to go deeper. Ask each other, 'what are you *really* worried about? What are your concerns about us?' When we invite our spouse to know our deepest concerns, fears and insecurities, we not only get to know each other in a deeper way, but we embrace the opportunity for healing to take place.

Sexual problems are usually less about an actual lack of performance, and more about what that lack of performance means to you, to your self-esteem and to your partner.

It raises the questions:

Am I a good enough lover?

Can you still love me if I let you down?

How will you handle it when I disappoint you?

Do you see me as weak?

If I fail you, will you still love me? Will you stay around anyway?

Digging deeper into our dysfunction is a gift! It allows us to know our spouse and ourselves more fully.

Team Approach

Sexual dysfunction does not have to feel like a 'personal failure' that an individual partner must fix on their own. It's always a 'couple problem'—as it affects both partners individually, as well as their relationship. Sexual dysfunction requires a 'couple solution.'

Every now and then, clients come to my office on their own, wanting help with their sexual problem. They feel like whatever is wrong, it is their problem, and therefore their responsibility to 'fix it.' And although I willingly treat people individually (and sometimes that is the best approach at certain stages of treatment), working on solutions for sexual problems or dysfunction is far more effective when we face it with a 'team approach,' with both partners actively working together to find solutions.

It is often in the process of doing exercises together, exploring different ways to bring sexual pleasure and satisfaction to their intimacy, that a couple become empowered to communicate in a far more healthy and respectful way about sex. Together, they learn so much more about each other than if they had not had any sexual problems in the first place!

> **Talk together:**
>
> *What are we missing here? What can we do differently? How can we both be more relaxed, or have more fun, or bring more enjoyment to our intimacy? What are our fears that we are not talking about?*

Compromise

Sex isn't just about what you want—sex can be about both of you growing closer together. Remember, intimacy is always the goal.

Sex might not always be exactly the way you want it. That's compromise. Sex in your marriage needs to be about what works for both of you.

To find intimacy, joy and fulfilment, you need to learn to compromise and work together.

Sex takes work; it requires us to be flexible, to try different things, to do things in different ways, so that even if it is not your preferred or ideal experience, the outcome is still that your closeness, intimacy and connection as a couple, grows.

Focus on Sensual Connection

When you were dating or engaged, you both took time to 'go slow' and to touch each other with gentleness and affection. It wasn't a race to the finish line. You noticed things like your partner's scent, or how they looked—you noticed how the different clothes they wore created 'want' within you, or how the way they styled their hair made them more attractive to you. You were aware of every part of them, their touch, their taste, their smell, their voice, the way they looked. All five senses were awakened!

Remember the simple things you did to connect to each other, the fingers gliding down the inside of your arm, the whispering in each other's ears, the simple playing with your hair, the hand on yours, or the skin on your skin. All those moments of sensual touch made you feel relaxed, close and connected.

Sensual touch engages the five senses: hearing, touch, smell, taste and sight. Start with affectionate touching and gradually build up to pleasurable touching and then to sexual touching. Focus on being present in the moment without thinking about 'where is this going to lead?' and 'how are we going to end this?' Instead, slow things down, be present, and take the focus off performance.

Your Worth is More than your Sexual Performance

Your manhood is not based on the performance of your penis. Your womanhood is not based on your ability to achieve orgasm. That is what our social and cultural world view tells us. But there is so much more to you that your sexual performance.

> *'Do you not know that your bodies are temples of the Holy Spirit, who is in you, whom you have received from God? You are not your own; you were bought at a price. Therefore, honor God with your bodies.' 1 Corinthians 6.19-20 NIV*

You are a child of God, a son and daughter of the most high God. You are made in His image. You belong to Christ.

This truth is unchangeable and irreversible. You have been paid for with a high price. Your freedom, healing and wholeness were paid for by Jesus' blood. Your life is priceless! It holds incredible value. You are valuable because God says you are and because God showed you are, by sending Jesus to die in your place. Don't cheapen your value or worth by making it about how you perform.

Seek Professional Help

If you experience pain during sex, are unable to have intercourse, or find it hard to achieve or maintain an erection, you are not the only one. If you are struggling with pornography, past sexual abuse is affecting your intimacy, or as a couple, you don't know where to start in working through your intimacy challenges, seek medical and professional help. Medical specialists, sexual health professionals, sex therapists, and pelvic floor physiotherapists are specialised in this area and can provide effective treatment and helpful resources.

There is no shame in putting your hand up, so don't put off seeking help! The earlier you get help, the better for your marriage.

Hold onto Hope

There is no doubt that a person experiencing sexual dysfunction can feel like there is no hope for their situation. The thought of having hope can even feel scary—because, 'if things *don't* change, what does that mean for our relationship? What does that say about me?'

Thankfully, God has another point of view.

> *'For I know the plans I have for you,' says the Lord. 'They are plans for good and not for disaster, to give you a future and a hope.' Jeremiah 29:11 NLT*

If you are reading this book and feel hopeless about your situation, I encourage you to hold on to hope. God has a plan to bring hope to your future!

- Discussion Questions for Couples -

Growing up, how did your parents refer to genitals?

How can I know when you are aroused (aside from the physical response of lubrication or erection)?

Do you need to experience orgasm for your sexual intimacy to be satisfying and fulfilling?

What is a turn on and a turn off for you?

What can I do to build your desire?

3.
THE BEAUTY AND WONDER OF YOUR SEXUALITY

Embracing the gift of physical intimacy

As a teenager, I vaguely recall a sex education class where we were taught about putting something on a banana. Did anyone else have that class?! I remember learning about menstruation and periods—and that was it. There was nothing on values about sex and relationships, nothing about how to understand sexual feelings or thoughts, and definitely nothing about how to navigate relationships and intimacy. *Intimacy?* That word was not even mentioned. Who would have thought it had anything to do with sex and relationships?!

But like every teenage girl with a changing body and a developing interest in boys, I was curious! What was it like to kiss someone? What did sex feel like? What should I do if a boy made a move on me? There was so much my friends and I were 'wondering' but had no idea who to ask.

Thank God for teen girl magazines—especially the sealed sections! When my girlfriends and I hung out at each other's places, we would read our copies of *Dolly* and *Girlfriend*. At the back of every *Dolly* magazine was a section called 'Dolly Doctor,' where teenage girls could ask questions about sex, periods, puberty, and dating, and 'Dolly Doctor' would give the answer.

Soon, we moved on to the sealed 'sex section' of *Cosmopolitan* and *Cleo*. We hankered for more in-depth education. We were full of curiosity, we were hungry to learn, and those magazines gave us our 'sex and relationships' education. Back then, there was no internet or Google, and we certainly weren't going to talk to our parents!

And so, through what I learned from magazines, combined with my friends' (and my own) personal experiences of guys and relationships, my personal belief systems about sex and relationships were formed. Needless to say, they weren't exactly healthy!

VALUES AND BELIEFS ABOUT SEX

Many parents think they don't need to talk to their kids about sex, that they will figure it out themselves—and that's exactly what many of us did as teenagers. We figured it out by ourselves, in secret, feeling awkward and embarrassed. The only message we got as kids was that 'sex is a secret, we should be ashamed of it, and we shouldn't talk to anyone about it.' Wouldn't it be awesome if learning about sex was not something that we had to figure out on our own, but was openly discussed with people we love and trust?

> **Talk together:**
>
> *What was your experience of puberty? What messages about sex were you taught? Were they generally positive or negative? What did you wish you knew more about? Were your questions openly received and answered?*

There are many experiences in our lives that contribute to forming our understanding of sexuality—the way we were raised as a child, how love and affection were displayed in our families, how safe we felt to express emotions and vulnerabilities, and how we were taught about sex (not just the basics, but about our anatomy and how our body works). Even our experience of becoming an adolescent and going through puberty contributes to the way we understand our sexuality, as do our past and current sexual experiences.

Our values, attitudes and beliefs about sex and relationships are formed through our family of origin (how we were raised, our childhood and adolescent experiences), our religion and faith, and our culture and society. And often, we don't realise the influence and impact these messages have in forming a positive or negative, healthy or unhealthy, perspective on sex.

I have two brothers (one who is my twin), and I am the only girl in my family. I grew up with boys around me all the time—which is definitely a healthy thing! I still remember spending most of my weekends as a kid and teenager at the soccer field, watching my brothers play soccer. Having a twin brother meant that we spent a lot of time with each other's friends; by default we had our own girl-guy friendship group, and I'm sure all our friends loved it! But having friends that were guys meant that I heard their conversations about girls, and what they could get from them sexually. This led me to form the unconscious belief that all a guy wants from a girl, is sex.

> **Talk together:**
>
> *Which unhealthy comments or beliefs have you heard about sex?*
>
> - *You shouldn't have sexual desire outside of marriage.*
> - *Genitals are dirty and you should not even look at them.*
> - *If you like sex, you must be a _____ .*
> - *If you don't 'try before you buy' how will you know if someone is good in bed?*
> - *Your spouse will satisfy your every sexual desire.*
> - *If you don't give sex regularly, your partner will leave you.*
> - *Sexual desire can't be controlled.*
> - *I've made mistakes in my past, so I don't deserve a good sex life.*

By identifying and addressing unhealthy belief systems about sex and relationships, we can begin to experience the joy and freedom that sex in marriage was intended to give us. If we don't, it has the potential to affect our sexual relationship in marriage. We may not desire sex, we might not enjoy sex, or we may avoid sex.

We live in a highly sexualised world where sex is idolised. Our culture is full of sexualised images, innuendo and advertising. Our society promotes and celebrates loveless sex. This worldview frames and influences our personal views on sex, and even though our world is highly sexualised, sex remains a strangely taboo subject, one that we find it difficult to talk about on a personal level.

Some of us have experienced things in our past that were abusive, destructive and just plain *not right*. I am so sorry for this. You did not deserve it, and it is not your fault. Some of us have been exposed to pornography or have developed a habit or addiction to pornography and masturbation. These experiences bring us emotional pain, shame, and guilt; but they can also impact how we relate in our intimate relationships. These experiences can make talking about sex even more challenging. I urge you to be brave! Courageously talk to a trusted friend or a health professional; seek guidance on how to find healing and wholeness from your past. It may be a journey—but the journey to wholeness and freedom is always worth it.

You see, God is the designer and creator of sex, relationships and intimacy. He has a plan and a purpose for our sexuality that is so much more than rules or 'do's and don'ts.' We need to explore the *why* behind His great plan for sex. We need to explore what we believe and value, and we need to unpack the negative messages we have taken onboard. As we address unhealthy beliefs, we are able to develop a positive, healthy and God-honouring understanding about God's plan for our sexuality.

YOU ARE A SEXUAL BEING

Alana grew up as the only girl in a strict religious family with three brothers. Her parents hardly spoke to her about sex, but they often made comments about her friends or other women in their town. 'She needs to keep her legs shut,' they would say. 'No guy will want her now that she has broken up with her fiancé.' Alana was taught to cover up her body, to not reveal too much in case the boys at youth group 'stumbled' or started to think of her in a sexual way. But Alana developed a relationship with a guy she found very attractive. It seemed strange, that she should feel so attracted to him, but she liked the new feelings.

Their relationship progressed well, and recently they got married. Both Alana and her husband chose to wait until they were married before having sex and being intimate together. However, since the wedding, Alana has viewed sex as something she has to do for her husband, something that is right for their marriage 'because that's God's plan for sex.' But for her? Alana doesn't see sex as something for her or as something she wants or enjoys. Sex is not something she is comfortable doing for her own pleasure. Alana struggles to give herself permission to experience the beauty of sex for herself.

'I am a sexual being.' How comfortable are you with thinking of yourself this way? Be honest. How do you feel about enjoying sex for yourself? How do you feel about experiencing desire and arousal with your spouse, or being vulnerable and seen intimately by your spouse? How we think makes all the difference. We are created as sexual beings. Contrary to belief, our biggest sex organ is not our genitals—it's our brain! Our brain is where we experience love, pleasure and intimacy.

When you think about your sexuality, is it in a positive or negative way? Are you confused or unsure about how to understand your sexuality? How we perceive and make sense of our sexuality is influenced by the positive and negative messages we receive from our social culture, cultural background, childhood upbringing and religious upbringing.

DESTRUCTIVE MESSAGING

Female Sexuality

It is no wonder that women find it difficult to accept and appreciate that they are sexual beings. For some women, simply saying, 'I am a sexual being' fills them with great embarrassment and shame. But God did not leave female pleasure out of His design for sex! In fact, the clitoris' sole and only purpose is to bring a woman pleasure! Why would God create the clitoris if sex wasn't meant to be pleasurable for a woman?

And yet, our education systems have taught teenagers that puberty equals wet dreams and erections for boys, and periods and pregnancy for girls. Masturbation as an adolescent is normalised for boys, but there is little mention of masturbation for girls. In such messages, the concept of pleasure for women has been undermined.

On top of that, women have often heard a message of guilt. In many societies, there is social stigma around girls wearing certain clothing, as if what they wear equates to 'asking for abuse.' When sexual correctness is valued over sexual fulfillment, the result is stifling to a woman. In many cultures, a woman's role in sex has been confined to duty and a sense of obligation to satisfy the man. Conservative cultures that promote an ignorant or fear-based message about sex, are always destructive to a woman's sexual self-esteem.

Society has also accepted pornography as a normal part of sexuality. Pornography is essentially where young people get their sex education, yet its message is degrading towards women; it is racist, violent, distorted, and reinforces the idea of a one-size-fits-all type of body without ever displaying intimacy, safety, respect, communication or consent.

The message is still being given that the vagina is dirty, that it is the portal that gets a girl into trouble (loss of virginity, unwanted pregnancy, sexually transmitted diseases etc) and therefore it needs to be closed up, and not exposed. The prevalent message is, 'be fearful of it!' Cultural practices such as female genital mutilation are essentially about controlling female sexuality under the guise of the belief that preventing a woman from experiencing pleasure guarantees that she will remain a virgin for her one-day husband.

The result is that many women are not comfortable in their own body, are ashamed to experience pleasure, feel embarrassed about their genitals, lack confidence in their sexual expression and are ignorant of their anatomy and how their sexual functioning works.

Male Sexuality

Society and culture have likewise indoctrinated men with ideas of their anatomy, physiology and sexuality that are misguided, unrealistic and often destructive. One big example, pardon the pun, is a man's penis size. While men might freely swing them around in locker rooms and claim that they don't look at each other's size, they can't deny the feeling that size does matter and that 'bigger is always better.' Penis size can create significant anxiety for males. As we know, flaccid and erect penis's vary in size, and size has no impact on a male's sexual function. A bigger penis does not necessarily make a woman orgasmic during intercourse because it is the clitoris, not the vagina, that is the woman's main organ for pleasure. Regardless, most women would probably prefer to not have a big penis inside them anyway! This ridiculous focus on size can make men feel insecure, inadequate and unconfident. The antidote to this is to de-bust the myth, love your body and accept your penis! Remember, *'it's not about the size of the boat, it's about the motion of the ocean!'*

Another destructive dominant message from our society is about a male's performance. A man is expected to perform at work, in his career, in his studies, in his sports, in his finances, in material wealth—and often, in the bedroom. Pornography hasn't helped the cause by depicting males with large penises and the ability to sustain an erection for extended lengths of time. Men need to liberate themselves from these unrealistic standards.

A WORD TO WOMEN

Your Magnificent Genitals

What narrative do you have about your vagina? With so much shame around female genitalia and female pleasure, many women have never even looked at their own vulva! Some fear putting anything into their vagina, even a tampon. Others have attached derogatory names towards their vulva—words like, *dirty, gross, smelly* and *ugly*.

Our culture has not taught people to treat vulvas with care, sensitivity and privilege. It is not surprising to hear that a woman is not comfortable with her own beautiful body parts. In many ways, we have become convinced that something God created and declared good, perfect and beautiful, is, in fact, ugly. The truth is, the enemy has fed us lies, and many of us have sadly, and destructively, taken them onboard.

But there is beauty and wonder to your genitals. Vaginas and vulvas are delicate, sensitive, and a magnificent piece of the female anatomy. The vagina can expand to fit a penis *and* to enable a baby to come out. It gives pleasure, *and* it gives life!

The vagina envelopes, accommodates and comforts the penis, bringing pleasure not only to the penis, but to the soul, spirit, heart, mind and body of the man. And, it welcomes the seed of new life, birthing the next generation of incredible people who will impact the world. No other organ can do that!

How powerful, giving and resilient the female genitals are!

Embrace Your Body

Your body is your friend, not your rival. How do you treat your body? Always treat your body with kindness, encouragement and love. It does so much to help you enjoy your life and live out your purpose. You cannot enjoy a healthy sexuality if you cannot embrace your body. Your body is beautiful! And, your body is designed to represent Christ.

So, love and embrace your body. It's the only one you have! Don't focus on what you don't have; instead, own what you do have—the size, the wrinkles and the curves. You are created a sexual being and *you are sexy!* Confidence is attractive, so be confident in your own skin by accepting and loving who you are.

Ladies, whatever you are self-conscious about, it is more than likely that your man has not even noticed or doesn't even care. A woman may be worried about the cellulite on her buttocks, while her husband hasn't even noticed her wobbly behind. He is just 'peaking' at the fact that she is beautiful and stunning in her nakedness. It is that simple. Take the pressure and worry off and give yourself permission to embrace your body and your sexuality as you are.

Song of Songs is a book that is dominated by the woman's voice, seeking, pursuing, initiating and exclaiming her physical attraction to her man. It is full of beautiful imagery of two people aroused, shame-free, confident and full of joy in each other's sexuality.[1]

> 'My beloved is radiant and ruddy, outstanding among ten thousand. His head is purest gold; his hair is wavy and black as a raven. His eyes are like doves by the water streams, washed in milk, mounted like jewels. His cheeks are like beds of spice yielding perfume. His lips are like lilies dripping with myrrh. His arms are rods of gold set with topaz. His body is like polished ivory decorated with lapis lazuli. His legs are pillars of marble set on bases of pure gold. His appearance is like Lebanon, choice as its cedars. His mouth is sweetness itself; he is altogether lovely. This is my beloved, this is my friend, daughters of Jerusalem.' Song of Songs 5.10-16 NIV

If you want that kind of relationship with your sexuality, it's important to bring your perspective in line with God's! *How does God see you? How does God want you to see your sexuality?* Start speaking His affirmations and truths over yourself.

It doesn't matter if it sounds unnatural at first—as you persist in affirming the wonder of your personal sexuality, your mind and heart will begin to respond! You don't even need to believe it to start speaking it!

Here are some affirmations:

- I am a sexual being. This is a wonderful part of who I am.
- My sexual desire is natural and healthy.
- I have been created to enjoy sex. Pleasure and orgasms are God-created and a gift for me to enjoy.

---

[1] D Allender & T Longman III, Intimate Allies, Tyndale House, 1999, 253-54

- My genitals are normal, beautiful and perfect. They are able to bring me pleasure.

- I am secure and comfortable in my body. I celebrate my sexuality with my spouse.

- My vagina is good, perfect and beautiful. My vagina is flexible and stretchy. It is capable of holding a penis snugly inside and expanding to birth a baby.

- My clitoris was created with the purpose to enjoy sexual pleasure and satisfaction.

- My penis is strong, healthy and perfect.

- I love my body and how it brings me and my spouse delight and pleasure.

- I am capable of being a great lover and giving my spouse pleasure.

- I give myself permission to let go and experience pleasure.

- Sexual intimacy with my spouse is healing, caring and nurturing.

THE BEAUTY AND WONDER OF SEXUALITY

There is a beauty and tenderness to sex—the soft tender kisses, the gentle caressing, the intense passion of wanting, the deep awakening of arousal, the intoxication of pleasure, the gradual relaxing and letting down of walls, the letting go of the cares of the world, the layers peeled back, the welcome to be comforted and nurtured, the closest place you can get to someone, the raw state of beauty and wonder . . .

Being invited into someone's most intimate space is an incredible privilege and honour. Sexuality is a private beaconing to your lover 'to come away with me and be a part of me.' It is erotic, sensual, pleasurable, unveiling, intimate, revealing, all-encompassing, and in the moment, it takes over every part of you with its pleasure and delight. But it is something you must choose, want and yield to fully.

The beauty and wonder of sexuality originated back in Eden. Adam and Eve, who were naked and felt no shame, explored the beauty and wonder of being seen, deeply known, and intensely consumed with perfect delight and wonderful pleasure. Awaken the beauty and wonder of your sexuality in your marriage! Your sexuality is erotic and pleasurable, deep and powerful. Don't settle for a superficial, cheapened, worldview of sex!

- Discussion Questions for Couples -

Do you see yourself as a sexual being?

What does sex mean to you personally?

What beliefs and values have you developed about your sexuality?

What dominant messages did you grow up with about boys and girls, men and women?

How was affection and connection modelled to you in your family?

What was your experience of going through puberty? What was talked about or avoided? Were you confused about things?

What did you wish you knew more about? Were your questions openly received and answered?

What messages about sex were you taught growing up? How have your experiences shaped how you see your sexuality?

How do you feel about enjoying sex for yourself? How comfortable are you with being vulnerable and seen by me?

Do you think you deserve to experience pleasure in our marital sexual intimacy?

4.
YOUR PRIVATE PARADISE

Awakening and exploring
pleasure in intimacy

'I want to love all the parts of you.'

What a beautiful thought! As lovers, you have full permission to awaken and explore the private paradise of intimacy and pleasure within your marriage.

> *'My darling bride, my **private paradise**, fastened to my heart. A secret spring are you that no one else can have—my bubbling fountain hidden from public view. What a perfect partner to me now that I have you.'* Song of Songs 4.12 TPT

SEX TAKES WORK

Sexual intimacy is, indeed, like entering a private paradise. But like any garden, it needs to be cultivated. Sex takes work! Many people have the assumption that sex will just happen, that it is natural and that everything will just work. We get this view from the movies—a couple starts kissing, within seconds the woman is highly aroused, and seconds later, they are both climaxing together! You never see a couple on the screen fumbling around, figuring out a position that works, even if the couple are different heights! And even when we talk to our friends, it is very rare that we share the difficulties or challenges we face as we try to get sex to work in our marriages.

One thing is for sure—your first experience of intercourse is probably not going to be the best sex you will ever have, because sexual intimacy gets better as you continue to work at it together! You are not born a good lover! You make yourself a good lover through practice, learning and experience. There will be times where you will have the most amazing sexual experiences and other times when it's just plain average. Don't freak out, this is totally normal. You are not a machine, so make sure your expectations about sex are realistic.

When Sally and John got married, Sally was a virgin. John, however, had a vibrant and active sexual past with multiple sexual partners before he met Sally. This made Sally insecure. She was worried that she wouldn't compare to John's past sexual partners. This fear of being 'not good enough' in bed made her lack confidence in the bedroom.

Your past sexual experience doesn't make you a sex expert, or an expert on your spouse's sexuality. You might know a few techniques or have had many experiences, but what you and your spouse create, build and enjoy together is unique to the two of you. No two people are the same. So, leave your past experiences at the door and go into your marriage with curiosity and an openness to learn about and know each other.

Let's explore different types of pleasurable sexual touch:

FOREPLAY

'You cannot work at creating better lovemaking – you and your partner have to play at it.'

Foreplay is the mental, physical and sexual acts that create desire, build anticipation and stimulate arousal. To create pleasure and experience satisfaction in your lovemaking, you need to start with foreplay.

Foreplay is the creative, fun, playful part of your relationship. The word, 'play,' in 'foreplay' tells us it's meant to be fun. Foreplay makes the play last longer, and it makes it more enjoyable for both of you. It can lead to longer sex and better orgasms.

Your bodies are a playground for each other to enjoy. It takes more than a few quick minutes of kissing or genital touching before intercourse. Great foreplay might include caressing your spouse's hair, kissing their neck, whispering in their ear, sharing a bath or shower together, washing each other's bodies, using body oils to give each other a massage, holding hands, hugging, soft slow kisses, cuddling, playing some music, lighting candles, delivering flowers, leaving love notes around the house, teasing or flirting with each other, dancing with clothes on or off, sharing each other's fantasies, dressing up or role playing, playing games like strip poker or naked twister, cooking dinner in just an apron, heels or a bow tie (provided you don't have kids in the house!), caressing each other's bodies, and exploring different ways of touching or giving oral genital stimulation.

Texting is a great way to build erotic anticipation. You can often be more graphic in a text than you might feel like being in person. Write something with lipstick on the bathroom mirror at the start of the day. Make your bedroom inviting, dim the lights, put some fresh, smooth sheets on the bed, turn on some music and light some aromatic candles. Go to bed naked or wear some sexy underwear. The options are endless when you get creative! Yes, it may take effort and thought, but this is an investment into your relationship and a way of placing value on your spouse. Your spouse and your relationship are worth the effort.

Don't shorten or limit foreplay to only a few minutes or seconds before intercourse. Foreplay should be twenty to thirty minutes of closeness and sensual touch, followed by twenty to thirty minutes of genital touch, stimulating arousal. This is a guide, rather than a rule, but if getting out the timer might help you, go for it!

Don't limit foreplay to what you do before the 'main event' of intercourse or what you do to get your partner ready for intercourse. Although it is preparation for intercourse, foreplay or 'sex outside of intercourse' can also be the 'main event!' Your sexual intimacy does not always have to end with intercourse.

Finally, foreplay starts in the morning. Every time you turn towards each other to connect, every time you lean in to share what you admire or appreciate about your spouse, you are building connection and closeness in your relationship. Every time you compliment your partner or tell them what you love or find sexy about them, you place value on your relationship.

Relationship researcher John Gottman says, 'every positive thing you do in your relationship is foreplay.' Sex can be an all-day affair! Exploring each other's bodies extensively includes all sorts of sexual acts.

STIMULATING BREASTS AND NIPPLES

Breasts (and especially the nipples) are erotically sensitive in both sexes. Both men and women can enjoy having their breasts or nipples stimulated, and some women can even experience orgasm from nipple stimulation.

Women usually prefer several minutes of body contact and gentle caressing before their partner kisses their breasts or sucks or licks their nipples. So start off slowly, with gentle caressing. When she is highly aroused, the woman may find hard sucking of the breasts or nipples to be enjoyable. Every woman's preferences are different though, so check with her to ensure the sucking is not hurting her, even if you are enjoying it.

A woman can stimulate her man's breasts or nipples by kissing, sucking, or licking, or by gliding over, rubbing or gently squeezing his nipples with her fingers. This additional stimulation can build his arousal and pleasure in the lead up to (or during) orgasm.

CARESSING GENITALS

Males and females may have different preferences when it comes to genital touch. Men may prefer their penis directly stroked at the start of foreplay. Women may desire intimate physical affection first such as hugging each other, caressing and massaging other parts of their body before stimulating and arousing the vulva. As you try different forms of touch, and talk about it together, you will understand more about the sort of touch that is arousing and erotic for you and your spouse.

'HERS'

Use lubricant to touch the vulva—it makes the sensations more arousing, but remember to not go straight for the clitoris or vagina. Instead, start with gentle rubbing of the inner thighs, moving to the pubic area. Stroke or make circular movements over the mons pubis. Women may enjoy firm pressure or massage from the palm of the hand against the mons pubis to stimulate the clitoral nerve endings.

Use your fingers to gently and rhythmically stroke the labia majora and labia minora and around the vaginal opening. The clitoris is the most sensitive structure in the female body. Due to its sensitivity, the clitoris needs careful and delicate stimulation to result in sexual arousal. Gently touch the clitoral hood from the top downwards, to protect the sensitive tip, the clitoris glans. The clitoral glans is so sensitive that some women cannot bear any direct touch to the glans. In that case, caressing around the clitoral glans can be more enjoyable.

You can gently touch the clitoris or the area around the clitoris, using circular motions such as drawing circles or figure 8's, or by caressing up and down or side to side. You can also build arousal and 'tease' the clitoris by focusing on it first and then focusing around it, or touching the labia lips, the mons pubis, or the perineum, and then going back to the clitoris. The teasing of going back and forth builds tension in the woman.

Rubbing your penis against the clitoris or rubbing it up and down the outside of the vulva can also be arousing for her. Apply more lubrication when needed, then, when she is aroused, try inserting a finger or two into the vagina, focusing on stroking the vaginal entry and the outer third of the vagina. Finger and penis-penetration are more enjoyable to the women when she is already aroused, so make sure this is not the first touch made to the genitals. The top front wall of the vagina, between the urethra and vagina, known as the G-spot is the most sensitive. Gently touch this area in a circular motion and as arousal increases, you can increase the pressure.

If your wife does not enjoy gentle finger penetration, it may be because she is not aroused enough. Stop and go back to gently touching her vulva. Avoid deep, fast thrusting of the fingers inside her unless she is highly aroused, as it may not be enjoyable for her. The inner two thirds of the vagina are less sensitive as they have a small amount of nerve endings.

As arousal increases, the speed and pressure of touch can increase; then, when she is ready for orgasm, focus more intensely on clitoral stimulation. Some women prefer that their partners stop stroking while they are experiencing orgasm, others enjoy continued stimulation. You can communicate to your spouse through physically guiding their hands, or by telling them your preferences.

A man's penis is not the only way to bring a woman pleasure. His penis size does not determine his wife's enjoyment of sex. The stimulation of the clitoris is what brings a woman pleasure. It is normal for women to experience orgasm through masturbation or oral sex but not through penis-vagina intercourse. However, orgasm during intercourse can be experienced with additional manual stimulation of the clitoris.

'HIS'

Start slowly by gently touching and caressing the hips, pelvic area, inner thighs and pubic hair above the penis. Stroke his perineum and massage the scrotum. To reduce friction and make genital touch more enjoyable, use personal lubricant on your hands and on his penis. Saliva can be an alternative to lubricant. Remember that when there is not enough lubrication, friction can be painful and uncomfortable.

Firmly wrap one hand around the shaft and frenulum of the penis, and engage in slow, soft stroking of the penis with up and down movements, changing the speed and pressure as he becomes more aroused. Use the other hand to continue to caress the scrotum or massage the perineum to enhance arousal. You can focus on stroking and massaging the frenulum and corona of the penis, then move to the shaft and back again to add variety and enhance pleasure.

ORAL SEX

Oral sex can be a positive way to enhance each other's pleasure. It can be one of the most intimate ways of making love, as it provides your spouse with a direct view of the body parts that are commonly private and unseen. Yet, it is not uncommon for people to feel too embarrassed or shy to engage in oral sex.

Like any sexual act or touch, it is important that as a couple you openly discuss your feelings about engaging in oral sex.

'HERS'

The soft, warm and lubricated tongue provides intense stimulation and is often the best way or most consistent way for a woman to experience orgasm. She may also be more open to direct clitoral stimulation by a tongue. Begin by softly kissing the inner thighs, slowly drawing nearer to the vulva. Give little kisses around the labia majora and minora and the clitoris and try blowing gently on these areas of the vulva. Gradually lick upwards from the vaginal entrance—don't go straight for the clitoris or insert the tongue immediately into the vagina.

Try different ways of enhancing pleasure, such as gentle tugging, sucking, kissing, licking from the bottom up, in circular or figure-eight tongue movements. Involve the whole vulva, the labia majora, labia minora, vaginal opening, perineum and the clitoral region. The tongue inside the vagina can be soft and pleasurable. Further techniques about this type of intimacy, can be found in Ian Kerner's book, 'She Comes First.'[1]

'HIS'

Start slowly by kissing the head of the penis, followed by slow, tiny licks using the tip of your tongue. When the glans is in your mouth, swirl your tongue around. Pay special attention to the corona and frenulum, where the shaft meets the head of the penis, as this part of the penis is very sensitive and arousing. Licking the penis and moving it up and down in your mouth can be very stimulating. You can vary the speed of the motion, from slow to more intense, and vary the pressure from the muscles of the mouth and jaw. To enhance pleasure, you can use your

---

[1] I Kerner, She Comes First: The Thinking Man's Guide to Pleasuring a Woman, William Morrow, 2004

hands to stroke the shaft of the penis or fondle the scrotum while using your mouth to suck the head of the penis. Running a finger up and down the seam of the centre of the scrotum can be especially pleasurable. To prevent gagging, your wife can be on top when performing oral sex and hold the penis with both her hands to control the depth of penetration.

The 'sixty-nine' position enables both partners to give oral sex at the same time. In this arrangement, both partners are upside down and facing each other, either on top of each other or side by side, where they are able to experience simultaneous stimulation and pleasure. Some couples prefer taking it in turns to give and receive oral sex so that each partner can simply enjoy receiving or giving sexual pleasure. If the wife is not comfortable having her husband ejaculate in her mouth, she can ask him to pull his penis out of her mouth when he is close to ejaculation. And be assured—you cannot get pregnant (or fat!) by swallowing semen.

Many people enjoy performing and receiving oral sex, while other people find it makes them uncomfortable. If one partner wants it and the other partner doesn't like it or isn't comfortable doing it, navigate the topic respectfully, seeking flexibility and compromise. Engage in an open, non-defensive discussion. Seek to learn and understand what your partner thinks or is concerned about. This can help alleviate concerns or worries. Remember the best possible sexual intimacy is built on respect and trust.

SEXUAL INTERCOURSE

There are a variety of sexual positions you can try together. Experiment with different positions to discover how you best fit together, what you both enjoy and keep variety in what you do.

Below are some of the basics to start you off exploring:

Man on Top

Commonly referred to as the 'missionary' position, the woman lies on her back with her legs spread and the man lies in the middle of her legs and gently inserts his penis into her vagina. This position brings the couple together face to face which is great for intimacy—and, you are able to stay under the covers if the children accidentally walk in on you!

This position is simple and effective and highly stimulating to the man. With his freedom of movement, he can control the speed and strength of thrusting, making it more likely for him to ejaculate earlier. This position is not as pleasurable for the woman, however. While the man's pelvis does stimulate the woman's clitoris, without deep penetration, even if clitoral stimulation occurs, it may not be enough for orgasm.

Woman on Top

In this position, the man lies on his back, with the woman facing him, straddled over his pelvis, where she can guide his penis into her vagina. She can widen her knees or bring them in closer to his body; she is free to sit up or lie forward, rock up and down, or roll her pelvis around to create different sensations as she comes from different angles.

This position allows deep penetration for the wife, and her husband can manually stimulate the clitoris, breasts and nipples, intensifying her orgasm. As this position is less stimulating for the male, it helps him delay and control his orgasm. However, it can be visually arousing to have his partner in full view and watch her enjoy pleasure.

Side Entry

With side entry, both partners lie on their side facing the same direction. The woman is in front of the man with her top leg resting over the man's legs. The man then inserts his penis into her vagina from behind.

This position has a lot of skin contact and allows for slow, relaxing, prolonged sex, although deep penetration is limited. As both the husband and wife are lying on their side, neither partner needs to support their weight, and their hands can move freely to stimulate the clitoris. This is an ideal position for women who are pregnant or couples who are fatigued.

Rear Entry

With rear entry, the woman is on her hands and knees with her partner kneeling behind her, holding onto her hips. He then inserts his penis into her vagina from behind, where he can control the thrusting.

This is a great position, as the deep penetration of the vagina makes it easier to reach the G-spot and is highly stimulating for both partners. The man is able to thrust slow or fast, firmly or softly, while also touching his wife's body. The clitoris does not get direct contact from the penis in this position, however both partners' hands are free to stimulate the clitoris manually and simultaneously. As partners are not facing each other, however, this position can feel impersonal.

Most women need manual stimulation of the clitoris during intercourse to reach orgasm. In any sex position, if she or her partner can reach the clitoris, it can be stimulated while simultaneously penetrating the vagina.

AFTERPLAY

Afterplay is about maximising the moment before you roll over and go to sleep. It is an act that reinforces your attachment, connection and closeness. It could be holding each other, telling your spouse that you love them, having a cup of tea or a glass of wine together, cooking together or simply talking. Try it next time and see how it builds your intimacy!

INTIMATE ACTS

Many couples form assumptions that any intimate or sexual act needs to follow through or end with intercourse. *'If he kisses me, it means he wants to have sex'* or *'if I have a shower with her, we need to have sex,'* are common misconceptions.

Build a balance of non-sexual intimacy and sexual intimacy in your marriage so that you and your spouse do not develop a sense of pressure or expectation that anything you do physically must mean that sexual intercourse needs to follow. Of course, there will be times where intercourse or orgasms will follow, but it should not be a rule or expectation. Intimate acts such as looking deeply into each other's eyes, or massaging each other's feet or hands, are a great way to take the pressure off, making your connection more fun and enjoyable.

Consider which of these fun, non-sexual, intimate acts you may wish to build into your relationship:

Non-sexual intimate acts that can build your intimacy

- *Holding eye contact for longer than usual*
- *Whispering in your partner's ear*
- *Running your finger over your partner's lips, face, or stubble*
- *Kissing your spouse's nose or forehead*
- *Resting your head on your spouse's shoulder or chest*
- *Listening to their heartbeat*
- *Holding hands while sitting, walking or even when you are rushing somewhere!*
- *Cuddling or giving a hug from behind*
- *Sitting next to your partner with your legs touching*
- *Looking after each other when one of you is sick*
- *Sharing food with each other or letting your partner feed you*
- *Touching your partner's hair, chest or upper arms*
- *Giving your partner a hand or foot massage using lotion or oils*
- *Showering, bathing or swimming together*
- *Taking time to teach your spouse something*
- *Talking & listening to each other; writing love notes or poems*
- *Spending time in bed, drinking coffee, reading together or talking*
- *Dancing in your living room or going to a dance class together*
- *Playing romantic music or singing a love song to each other*
- *Sharing your hopes and dreams, fears and worries together*

Talk together:

What non-sexual intimate acts do you enjoy? What acts would you like to add to the list? Share them with your spouse.

Sexual, intimate acts that can spice up your 'play time'

- *A soft, long kiss at the start of your day*
- *Showering or bathing together, or washing each other's bodies*
- *Going to sleep naked*
- *Rubbing up against each other when clothed; 'Frottage' or 'dry humping.'*
- *An energetic make-out session with long stretches of kissing*
- *Stimulating the nipples and breasts with your mouth or hands*
- *Sexy talk with each other in person, in love notes, via text, or over the phone*
- *Oral sex (simultaneously or taking turns)*
- *Reading sexy stories to each other or writing one about you and your spouse*
- *Giving each other hand stimulation*
- *Buying each other sexy underwear and lingerie*
- *Playing sexy music before or when lovemaking*
- *Extending sexual pleasure by bringing yourself or your partner to the point of orgasm, then pulling back just before release*
- *Including whipped cream or chocolate sauce in your lovemaking*
- *Undressing each other slow and tenderly*
- *Playing games like strip poker or twister semi-naked or naked*
- *Dancing semi-naked or naked for your partner; dancing together*
- *Role-playing a love story; dressing up*
- *Using a mirror or keeping the light on during sex*
- *Trying new positions*
- *Telling your partner your fantasies*
- *Going on a date and 'picking up' your spouse*

> **Talk together:**
>
> *Which sexually intimate acts appeal to you? What would you like to add to the list? Do you need to experience orgasm for your sexual intimacy to be satisfying and fulfilling?*

SEX SHOULD BE REGULAR

To build your intimate bond in your marriage, you should be having regular physical and sexual intimacy. Physical contact, such as holding hands, kissing and touching, releases oxytocin, the bonding hormone. It can improve our mood for days, helping us stay calm. Holding hands, hugging, touching, and making out can reduce your stress hormones (cortisol) and increase your sense of relationship satisfaction.

Many people want to know how often couples usually engage in sex, so they can compare themselves to others. The answer is that sexual intimacy in your marriage should be regular and consistent, but the frequency of sex can vary depending on the busyness of your week or month, your schedules, whether you are travelling or in town, and whether you are on holidays or have family living with you.

How frequently you enjoy sexual intimacy is about what you as a couple are satisfied with. Some couples are satisfied with having sex once a week. Some couples need more regular sex to feel satisfied and bonded. The key is to focus on caring for each other's needs rather than worrying or comparing yourselves to others. The best way to know is to talk about it as a couple.

> **Talk together:**
>
> *How often do you want to have sex? Should we be 'doing it' more? (or less?) Are we having enough sex?*

SEX SHOULD BE GOOD

There is more to sex than intercourse and orgasms, and since perfect sex every time is unrealistic, good-enough sex is what couples should aim for. It is normal to have times when you celebrate exceptional sex, or relish good sex, or enjoy 'okay' sex . . . and it is normal to have other times when you accept mediocre sex, or address dysfunctional sex. You are not a machine. A sign of healthy couple sexuality is your ability to accept this and not overreact to negative experiences.[2]

You are an intimate sexual team, working together, learning together, exploring and experimenting together and having fun in the process. Make pleasure and satisfaction the focus rather than how frequently you are having sex, how you perform and whether you orgasmed.

MEN AND WOMEN ARE NOT THE SAME

The common analogy that you may have heard before is 'men are like microwaves and women are like crockpots.' It means we are different—what works for you is probably not what works for your spouse. That's the beauty of sex!

Sex is a dance with our partner that is learned; in the process, we discover more about our spouse in the most intimate way. We need to

---

[2] B McCarthy, Sex made simple: clinical strategies for sexual issues in therapy, PESI Publishing & Media, 2015.

stop expecting and assuming that our partner thinks about sex like we do or wants sex like we do. Appreciate and embrace that you and your spouse are made differently, and realise that it is your job to learn how your partner is different to you sexually.

Men are usually willing and ready to get straight into 'the playing.' For males, when sexual desire sets in, the body responds with sexual arousal (erection) and follows with orgasm (ejaculation). Sexual desire is necessary for genital arousal (erection). It is normal for erections to wax and wane during sexual intimacy.

Men are visual and are turned on by sight. If you are both comfortable and want to enhance arousal or try new things, you can add a mirror to your bedroom, leave a light on during intimacy, walk around naked, or take a longer time getting dressed in the morning to let your spouse look at you. Women need time to talk about their day and share what they are thinking, to feel connected and close. When she feels emotionally connected, listened to and understood by her spouse, the cares of the day fade away and she can find herself desiring to be close and intimate.

ENGAGED COUPLES

Practical Tips for the Wedding Night and Honeymoon

Leading up to the wedding, there are a number of ways you can prepare for a wonderful wedding night and honeymoon.

Start with these suggestions:

Physical Check Ups

Make the investment in finding a doctor that you are comfortable with to talk about your sexual health. If you have questions or concerns about your sexual health, genitalia, erections, vaginal pain, or yeast or bacterial infections, openly discuss this with your doctor. They are there to help you. If you have a past sexual history or have had unprotected sex, talk to your doctor about a sexual health check-up.

Sexually transmitted infections are spread during sexual contact (vaginal, anal, oral sex), and untreated sexually transmitted infections can cause a variety of problems. Some infections have silent symptoms, meaning, you have no symptoms, so you don't know you have an infection. Infections left untreated can cause infertility and health problems but most sexually transmitted infections are treatable and easily tested for. Remember, you are looking after your health and your spouse's health by having a sexual health check-up.

Contraception

If you are not planning to conceive straight after your wedding, discuss contraception options with your doctor and then agree together on the most effective and beneficial plan for both of you. Take individual responsibility for contraception; don't leave it up to your spouse or make excuses about why you can't use contraception. Some women take the brunt of the responsibility for contraception by being on the contraceptive pill for years because their husband doesn't find wearing a condom pleasurable. Take all factors into consideration, such as the side effects of medical contraception on a person's wellbeing and body in the short and long term, not just the pleasure factor.

Educate yourself on contraceptive options and how you can fall pregnant. For example, some people think the 'pull out method,' where the man pulls his penis out of the woman's vagina before he ejaculates, is a form of contraceptive. However, you can still get pregnant on pre-ejaculate, although it is not common.

Some women have a steady and consistent menstruation cycle, know exactly when they are fertile, and avoid having sex during their fertile periods. Outside of their fertile periods, they choose to not use contraception. Make sure you are well-informed by getting professional reproductive advice before choosing this contraception method.

Contraception and medications can influence sexual desire, particularly low sexual desire and vaginal dryness. Check with your doctor for any sexual side effects to the medications you are taking. Using a lubricant may be necessary.

Get to Know Yourself

It is important that you know your body so you are comfortable to share your body with your spouse. Generally, this is easier for men than for women, especially when it comes to genitals. That's because men have dangly parts that hang outside their body, parts they are used to looking at and touching. The social conditioning around the penis is generally positive.

For women, however, most of their genitalia is internal, and the social conditioning tends to say, 'don't look down there.' If a woman gets to know her vulva, however, she will find it much easier to let her spouse know it too! So women, get out a mirror and take an intimate look at your genitals. Know where your clitoris is so you can show and guide your husband. Experience for yourself what it feels like to touch the different parts of your vulva. Get orientated with your body! This is not masturbation—it is simply discovering and touching your own body. As we get to know our bodies, we can develop a positive appreciation towards them.

Exercise your Pelvic Floor

Your pelvic floor is a group of muscles and ligaments in your pelvis that is attached to your pubic bone at the front and stretches like a hammock to the tailbone at the back. Pelvic floor muscles support the bladder, bowel and uterus in women, and the bladder and bowel in men. These muscles play a significant role in sexual sensation and sexual functioning.

Pelvic floor muscles can be strengthened by doing pelvic floor muscle exercises (called, 'Kegel exercises'), squeezing the muscles as if you are stopping your urine flow mid-way or tensing the muscles to keep yourself from passing wind. Draw in all the muscles around your anus, urethra or vagina; count to eight, then let go and relax. Then repeat: *squeeze in, lift up, hold tight* and *let go*. You should notice the difference when the muscles are tightened and when you have let go. Once you have learned how to do these exercises, they can be done anytime, anywhere.

For women, relaxing and tightening your pelvic floor muscles during sexual activity enables smooth entry for the penis and less discomfort. If muscles are too tight and it is hard to relax them, sex may feel painful. Learning how to relax and contract your pelvic floor muscles during sexual activity can increase sexual sensations. For men, strengthening the pelvic floor muscles allows you to control your erections and orgasms, and prevent premature ejaculation.

YOUR WEDDING NIGHT

Discuss your Expectations

As a couple, write down your expectations for the first night and then discuss what you wrote together. Be clear and specific. *Do you want to go out to dinner? Have a bath? Dance to music? Do you want lights on or dimmed? Are there things you don't want to do on the wedding night?* If you can say what you would like or hope for, this gives each of you a realistic expectation for the night.

I am mindful that people reading this come to their wedding night with a variety of different experiences. Some couples have already had sex (either with each other or with previous partners), some couples are both virgins or have one partner who is a virgin on their wedding night.

Regardless of your experience before your wedding, your wedding night is a beautiful time together. There is a lot of excitement and expectation. It is also normal to feel nervous or apprehensive or scared of the experience. It is so important to *go slowly* and not run into the experience quickly with eager passion. Here are some things to explore and consider:

Set the Focus

Make the focus about enjoying each other's bodies. Take the pressure off. You don't have to have intercourse, achieve an orgasm or last a long time on your wedding night. You have the rest of your lives together to experience all those wonderful things.

Create the Atmosphere

Create a relaxing, calm atmosphere by focusing on sensations and sensuality. Consider how you can engage with each other's five senses. Set the atmosphere with champagne or wine, cheese and crackers, chocolates and strawberries, candles, music, good sheets and romantic lighting. A glass or two of wine or champagne can relax you both, get you comfortable being together and ease those excited nerves. Take a bath together—warm water, candles and music around the bathtub can build a soothing, relaxing and romantic atmosphere.

Prepare in Advance

Prepare for the night by packing lubricant, condoms, and massage oils. Go to the toilet before and after sex. Have a shower before you start getting intimate.

Slow it Down

Go slowly and take the time to get to know and learn about each other's bodies. This is the fun part. There is no rush for the finish line. 'Having sex' is so much more than intercourse. It involves being naked together, seeing each other's bodies, touching each other and learning how to get each other aroused. Undressing and revealing yourself to your lover is a sacred and beautiful act. Take great delight in sharing the private secrets of your body with your spouse.

Foreplay

Foreplay is an essential part of sexual intimacy that shouldn't be skipped or rushed, especially on the wedding night. It creates desire, and helps each other become comfortable, safe, and ready for intercourse. Spend time focusing on arousal, as that is a key step to being able to have intercourse. Have foreplay, don't just go straight to the breasts or the genitals.

Take at least twenty minutes to undress each other and massage each other's feet, hands or body using body oils. Gently cuddle and caress each other's body with fingers, kisses or licks, before going to the breasts and genitals. Spend time touching the outside of her vulva with the hand or tongue before touching the clitoris or entering her vagina.

Husband, gently slide your fingers inside her vagina. She can practice squeezing and relaxing her vagina muscles whilst your fingers are inside to build muscle control. Relaxing the vaginal muscles is helpful, particularly if she is anxious about sex as these muscles can tighten unintentionally. Make sure to use lubricant when you are touching the outside of her vulva and the inside of her vagina.

Putting fingers in the vagina as part of foreplay should only take place when she is already aroused. Don't push your fingers in and out or be fast or intense about it; this is not stimulating and doesn't help her get ready for intercourse. You can find her G-spot if she is on her back. This can be very arousing, but if it makes her want to go to bathroom, it's okay. You are in the right place—it's just that she is not aroused enough yet to enjoy it.

Intercourse

You should only have intercourse when *she* is ready. It's a vulnerable act to allow someone to be inside you. It's a privilege and honour. Let your wife tell you when she is ready—when she is highly aroused, just before she has an orgasm. Use lubricant as part of your whole lovemaking experience, not just for intercourse. When you are ready to have intercourse, apply lubricant on the penis and on the outside and inside of the vagina.

'Missionary style' with her on her back or with her 'on top' where she can guide the pace and depth of penetration are good positions for a first experience. The penis and vagina are designed for each other. Slowly guide the entry of your husband's penis into your vagina. Be extremely gentle and patient with each other.

Insertion can be done in small steps. Start with the tip of the penis, then when she is comfortable, slowly move in further. Let her take the lead on how far she is comfortable for the penis to go inside. If her pelvic floor muscles are too tight, or lubrication isn't enough, she may experience discomfort. Be prepared that penetration (initial or complete) may not happen straight away. This is not unusual.

Once the husband is completely inside her, pause and stay still in the moment. This gives her time to relax and become comfortable with the penis inside her vagina. You may experience premature ejaculation. This is normal when it feels so good and you are excited and nervous. If this happens, it is not a sign of failure. As a first lovemaking experience, your wife probably doesn't need you to last much longer. Remember you have the rest of your lives to experience all the breadth and depth of sexual intimacy together.

If the husband ejaculates during intercourse, ejaculate fluid will gradually trickle out of her vagina afterward. Have a small towel or tissues close by, and she may even prefer to wear a liner after sex.

If either of you are not comfortable experiencing penetration to orgasm on your wedding night, you can stimulate and arouse each other manually or orally. Experiencing orgasm may not happen the first time you are sexually intimate together. It is normal for it take a while to learn how to bring each other to orgasm. Take the pressure off. It is common for women to not experience orgasm unless the clitoris is directly stimulated. If the male can't touch the clitoris depending on the position you are in, it is okay to touch yourself to experience orgasm during intercourse. This is not masturbation.

Communicate

You may not both know where to touch each other and how to touch each other, or whether to use soft and gentle or firm pressure. This is an exciting time to explore together. Be willing to show each other and tell each other what is enjoyable. Give each other verbal positive feedback to build each other's confidence.

Laugh

We all know that the wedding night has expectations attached to it, but don't take yourself too seriously. Make it about having fun together rather than performing and getting 'everything right.' Laugh when it doesn't work, when things are uncomfortable, when positions feel awkward and when you make different sounds and noises. Laughing at embarrassing and awkward moments can bring you closer and strengthens your bond.

Be Present

Be fully in *your* experience, open your eyes and take in the beauty and wonder of your sensual and erotic experience. Resist being a spectator in sex and be completely present with each other. Avoid comparing it to other experiences or measuring it up against your personal hopes and expectations. Your intimacy is beautifully unique. Value it!

Connect Afterwards

Compliment each other and share what you loved about being together, how nice it felt and how special it was to share the moment together. If either of you are anxious, nervous or worried about something, this connection time afterwards could help calm their nerves and ease their thoughts.

Remember, whatever your experience was together, whether it was what you were expecting or whether it didn't go according to your plans, your first experience of sex is not going to be the greatest sex you will have. Sex gets better as you work at it and as you grow together, learning and loving each other.

YOUR HONEYMOON

Honeymoons are a special holiday that you will always remember and look back on fondly. It's a time for you as a new couple to break away from the routine of life, to relax and to get to know each other. You may prefer a holiday full of adventure and sightseeing, or you may like a slow, beach side, 'swinging in a hammock' type of holiday. Whatever you choose, ensure you plan time to slow down and relax, with a lot of 'down time' to enjoy each other.

On your honeymoon, you can create a culture and example for how sexual intimacy in your marriage can be for the years to come. Do you want your sexual intimacy to be fun, adventurous, playful? You can build that culture from the start, by making your intimacy on your honeymoon fun! Explore and discover, experiment and be playful.

> **Talk together:**
>
> *What are your expectations for the honeymoon? What are you comfortable or not comfortable doing sexually? Set realistic expectations together.*

As you look forward to your honeymoon, take the time to discuss ways you plan to allure and discover one another:

Seduce Me

How would you like to be enticed and lured away? How do you imagine it in your mind? Would you like a soft, subtle kiss on your cheek, a gentle back rub or a firm touch on your bottom? Would you like your spouse to strike a pose, wear something sexy and revealing or simply nothing at all? Would you like desirous energetic daring statements like 'I need you now!'? Would you like romance and flowers, or massages and compliments? Experiment to learn how to initiate the way your partner likes it.

What makes you feel confident and sexy around your spouse? Is it something you wear, how you walk into a room, a look your spouse gives you or the way your spouse speaks to you? As you enjoy your beautiful private paradise together, explore different ways to build each other's sexual confidence. Discover what makes them feel sexy and what seduction in your marriage can mean for you both.

Explore Me

Your honeymoon is the perfect time to explore and experiment together—and there are no limits to what you can do! Just make sure both of you are comfortable with everything you try.

Consider giving each other full, naked, front and back body massages using massage oils. Take turns exploring every part of your partner's body; focus your attention on what it feels like to touch and enjoy their body, before even touching the genitals.

Explore giving and receiving. Use this time to learn how to manually stimulate each other to orgasm. Lubricants are sweet, they come in different flavours and can be fun to use when exploring. Sounds and noises can also be especially erotic; just make sure you aren't 'faking' it. That can be really humiliating for your partner.

Try different positions and think of all the places you could have sex on your honeymoon—the shower or bath, kitchen table or couch . . ? I will leave the rest to your imagination! Just experiment—you don't need to get stuck doing the same thing every time. You might even create your own couple erotic language, a 'sexy talk' that is personal and private to you as a couple. Are there certain words you find personally exciting? If the words you use together are not degrading or offensive, go for it!

Play with Me

Sex, especially on your honeymoon, should not be a serious act. Being serious is for when you are working and not for when you are in the bedroom! Sex can become a serious act when you are focused on things working 'perfectly.' There is no such thing as perfect sex! So scrap that idea and focus on playing!

This is your holiday! Laugh at yourselves, be playful and silly. As you play with each other, you will learn how your body works sexually, what feels good, how your body responds, what builds your desire for sex and what gets you aroused. It is really helpful to talk during sex. Say 'I really like that' or take their hand and guide the touch. You can also help your spouse understand how pleasurable it feels by saying, 'that feels ok,' or 'That feels so good, keep going!' for example.

HONEYMOON EXPECTATIONS

We go into relationships with expectations about sex, and couples who have intentionally chosen to wait until marriage often bring greater personal expectations about sex into their marriage. That's why it's so important to discuss them together.

Here are some common expectations:

'Sex just happens'

Sex will not be instantly amazing, even if you have waited all your life for your wedding night. Sex takes work, like anything else in life. Yet many people have developed the belief that 'sex should just happen,' that 'we will just know what to do.'

The best skill a couple can develop is to learn how to have healthy conversations about their sex life. Most partners are worried about offending or hurting their partner's feelings. Some partners find it too vulnerable to even say what they want or need. So, be patient, encouraging, empowering and complimentary. Say what you prefer instead of what you don't like. Great sex is talked about and worked at. If you want the benefits of a great sex life, you need to work at it.

'We are going to have sex all the time'

It is so often assumed that 'when we get married, all we will be doing is having sex!' And for couples who have waited to be married before having sex, the expectation can be even greater! The reality is, that married couples are *not* 'always' having sex. They have lives to live, careers to build, dinners to cook, kids' butts to wipe!

Sexual intimacy is part of their relationship and it should be something a couple does regularly to stay close and connected. But it's not the only thing they do. Expectations of frequency of sex need to be openly communicated and not assumed. Take the pressure off 'how often' and put your focus on intimacy and connection.

'Sex is all about intercourse'

This is such a limited and rigid view of sex. It limits the options and the fun. There is so much more to sex than just intercourse. Be curious and flexible to the breadth and depth of options you can do together to build your sexual intimacy. Start a conversation with your spouse and make it about play, adventure and discovery.

'Now that I'm married, I won't face temptation'

There can be an expectation that marriage will fix all our insecurities. Unfortunately, this is not the case; in fact, more often than not, marriage will highlight your personal issues even more. Marriage is not a magic wand.

Temptation doesn't go away because you are married. We all need to take responsibility for our own soul and spirit. Keep guard over your heart and mind and be careful about what you are letting in. Build the muscle of self-control in your thought life. Make and keep your spouse the object of your affection.

'Sex should be just like the movies'

Many of us have an idea of what sex is 'meant' to look like, mainly because of what we see in the movies or pornography. We think sex means hot, erotic, uncontrollable desire where we are pushed up against the wall, our clothes are ripped off in one go and orgasms are happening within seconds. Thanks to the movies, we think this is what sex is meant to be like. And when we don't experience sex like this, we think 'what's wrong with me?' or 'why don't I have desire like that?'

Real life sex is not like that at all! It is messy and awkward, certain positions don't work or are uncomfortable, and you may have to break the flow and stop during the act to use protection. Post-sex, you might not just be there, lying together in each other's arms, because you need to run to the bathroom and clean up! Or your husband has drifted off into a deep sleep from post-sex bliss! 'Real life sex' may not be as seamless as the movies portray it to be, but it can still be beautiful, intimate and romantic!

- Discussion Questions for Couples -

What non-sexual intimate acts do you enjoy?

What acts would you like to add to the list of non-sexual intimate acts to try together?

Which sexually-intimate acts appeal to you?

What would you like to add to the list of sexual intimate acts to try together?

What are your expectations for our wedding night?

What are your expectations for the honeymoon?

What are you comfortable or not comfortable to do sexually?

What is your personal expectation of sex in our marriage?

5.
SEX CHATS

Developing your most powerful
sexual technique

'Communication is the most important 'sexual' technique.'

Sex is vulnerable, but talking about sex can be even more vulnerable! We find ourselves stumbling over our words, hesitating to say what we are thinking and unable to clearly articulate ourselves. But healthy sexual intimacy in marriage is built through communication. No-one's sex life is perfect, and you are not a mind reader! A satisfying sex life does not happen by fluke or chance. A satisfying sex life is built by investing yourself into understanding and learning about your spouse and learning to express yourself openly, honestly and directly.

Talking about sex is courageous. But as difficult as it may seem at the start, the more consistently you talk about it, the more comfortable you will become.

SEX CHATS: AS AN ENGAGED COUPLE

For couples who have chosen to wait for marriage to be sexually intimate, it is normal to be nervous. It's also common to have worries, concerns or fears about your sexual relationship.

Discussing the Past

A person's sexual experiences, either with past partners or with pornography, can have a personal impact on their partner. They might be worried about comparison—*will you compare their performance? Is their body attractive enough? Are they doing it 'right?'* This feeling of inadequacy can be heightened if their partner does not have a similar sexual past.

Whenever you are discussing your past with your partner, be wise about the information you share. Before you share about your past, consider, 'Will sharing this help to build my spouse's sexual confidence? Will this help both of us feel safe and confident in our sexual encounters together?' Not everyone would prefer to know the details—most of the time, simply telling your spouse the basic facts is sufficient.

If your partner is upset by your sexual history, listen to them and understand their emotions and concerns. Avoid getting defensive—it won't achieve anything. Keep the focus on how, as a couple, you can move beyond your past and build the type of relationship you both desire. And remember, if you have had previous sexual relationships, it is important to have a sexual health check, and to discuss this with your fiancé before you have sex together.

If you have been using pornography, or have other destructive habits or addictions, as difficult as it may be, you need to tell your fiancé. Being transparent with him or her builds trust. It is such a scary thing, to tell the person you love something that you are potentially ashamed of.

Many people with pornography habits or addictions avoid telling their partners. They are worried they will hurt their partner, that their partner will be disappointed in them, or might want to leave them. Or they silently hope that getting married will make the problem go away. But often the problem doesn't go away . . . and it can continue to be a problem many years into the marriage, which is often when their partner finds out.

Hiding a pornography habit or addiction is unfair to your partner. It brings hurt and pain and breaks the trust that has been built in your relationship. It's hard to trust and respect someone that is not honest. A healthy relationship has honesty as a core value.

Unresolved Trauma

Past trauma has many adverse effects on our physical and mental wellbeing. When trauma is unresolved, it can impact a person's ability to trust, feel safe and build secure attachments in adult relationships. Unresolved trauma can also impair a person's ability to be sexually intimate.

It would be beneficial to you and your relationship, to work through these unresolved issues with a trauma-informed therapist who can help you understand your story and how to process the past in a safe way. Your therapist can help you to become a more secure, well-functioning couple by working with you as you build a healthy bond with each other.

Resolving the past takes courage, but your wholeness is worth it, and so is your relationship. Consider the support you both need in order to find healing. What books or resources can you access? What trusted couples, pastors or leaders can you seek wise counsel from? What health professionals or counsellors can support you?

Feelings of Guilt, Shame or Fear about Sex

If you are worried about your spouse comparing you to their previous partners, you are probably focusing on performance and technique rather than intimacy and closeness. Fix your focus on what you are creating with each other, focus on building intimacy and connection.

Comparison is never going to help you be satisfied and enjoy the gift you have been given in your spouse. Remember, the grass is always greener where you water it! If insecurity, body image or shame impact your ability to enjoy healthy sexual intimacy, it could be beneficial to work with a professional therapist or counsellor.

SEX CHATS: AS A MARRIED COUPLE

Sex needs to be an ongoing dialogue in your marriage, not a one-off conversation. There is so much to talk about when it comes to sex! Our sexuality is the most sensitive part of our lives. We need to treat this part of our relationship with sensitivity, compassion and dignity.

My work with couples has shown me how difficult is it for couples to talk about their sexual intimacy with each other. This is understandable, of course. We worry that we might hurt or offend our partner, and often we do not know how to clearly articulate what we are trying to say. Sometimes we are confused about what we even want. Consequently, we say nothing. We keep it all inside and we create internal assumptions about what we think our spouse is thinking and feeling. Let me share some of these:

'He hasn't initiated sex for ages; maybe he doesn't find me attractive.'

'She rejected me last three time; I guess she doesn't want me.'

'Since I've given birth, it's not the same down there for him.'

'He watches porn because I'm not good enough for him.'

This is unhealthy for you and for your relationship and is often not what your partner is thinking or feeling. The best thing to do with internal assumptions is to tell your partner what you are worried or concerned about and ask them for their perspective on the situation.

When sex is kept 'on the table' for discussion in your relationship, it makes it easier to bring up things that you would otherwise avoid or keep to yourself. The safest place to have this chat is outside of the bedroom. It is far less vulnerable to talk about sex over a cup of tea in the lounge room, with your clothes on.

It's so funny how when we are young and in love, we think 'my partner loves me and is going to know what to do to make me happy.' Hollywood-style romantic comedies show a love-struck man confessing his devotion to his woman saying, 'all I want to do is see you happy and make you smile.' These scenes lead us to believe that real love is demonstrated by a devoted partner who knows exactly how to make you happy (without even needing to be told by you).

I remember in the first years of our marriage, thinking 'he should know I like this' or 'he should know that talking is important to me.' I lived with the assumption that 'if you love me, you should just know what I like and what I need, and I shouldn't have to tell you.' Don't you think mind-reading would be such a helpful skill for marriage?! Unfortunately, my husband does not have telepathic powers. He does not know my thoughts or what I need. I have to tell him.

Thinking, 'you should just know, I shouldn't have to tell you,' is a ridiculous assumption. It breeds self-convenience. We excuse ourselves from having to do anything or make any effort to communicate. We blame our spouse or think it's their responsibility to figure out what we need. But your spouse doesn't know what to change unless you communicate openly. Your spouse does not know what you are thinking or what you want unless you tell them and show them. God did not create us to be mind-readers.

To have a great sex life, you need to put the investment into building healthy communication with each other. Some suggestions of ways to build communication about sex are:

Schedule a Weekly Sex Chat

A weekly ongoing chat helps keep sex 'on the table'; it keeps sex a priority in your marriage when it is something you consistently talk about. It allows differences to be brought up and stops the disappointment and resentment that come from unresolved issues. We often miss our partner's bids for connection during the week, and open discussion allows each partner to learn more about them and their inner world.

Here are some talking points that will help you get started:

'How have you felt connected to me this week?'

'What did I do or say that made us feel close this week?'

'Have there been times this week where you have desired to be close, physically or emotionally and we have missed each other, or it didn't happen?'

'Do you feel comfortable to share your desire to be intimate with me?'

'What are some things I can do to help you open up more with me about this?'

'Do you worry you will be rejected if you tell me your wants or desires?'

'How can we create comfortable and regular ways to discuss sex?'

'What feels good for you?'

'What part of our lovemaking did you enjoy the most?'

'How does our sexual intimacy make you feel?'

'How can I pleasure you more?'

Playful Nicknames

Some couples like to give each other's sexual parts playful nicknames. If this is a form of fun that you want to incorporate into your marriage, make the nickname affirming and loving. Sarcasm and criticism are not playful.

Use Gentle and Encouraging words

As talking about sexual intimacy is incredibly vulnerable, be intentional about building safety and respect in your communication. Speak to each other in love and use complimentary words. Frame your words with gentleness and kindness. For example, saying 'No! Stop! Don't touch me there!' can come across quite harsh and hurtful, while, 'It feels really nice when you touch me here,' or 'I'd like you to keep doing that for longer, it feels really good,' is feedback framed with positive encouragement.

The conversation is about understanding each other better, not pointing out what is not good or what is not happening.

Be Direct and Specific

When talking about your sexual needs, don't be vague, indirect, imprecise or inconclusive. Don't avoid rushing to the end of the conversation simply because you feel embarrassed or awkward—it makes it hard for your partner to decipher what you are really trying to say. If there is something you enjoy, tell your spouse through words, sounds or actions. 'I really like how we started kissing and touching on the couch first,' for example. This sort of talk builds your spouse's confidence, makes them feel secure as a lover and gives them insight into what your preferences are.

Hear Your Partner

Listening and hearing your partner reflects respect and honour. Pay careful attention when your spouse tells you that they don't like something. Don't assume that you know what works best for them. Ask them and then hear what they say. When you touch your partner, check in to make sure they are comfortable or if it is enjoyable for them. If they aren't enjoying themselves, enquire about what they need or what you can do to enable them to find it enjoyable.

Encourage Honesty

Partners can be scared to speak up about something they might like to do together or something that they are not enjoying. They are afraid they will offend their spouse or hurt their spouse's feelings. Instead, they keep quiet, even if it is unenjoyable or painful for them. This can build resentment over time. Offense and resentment are not conducive to intimacy. Decide you will not be offended. Welcoming feedback enables you to learn how to be a better lover.

Faking anything is hurtful, but this is especially true for orgasms. Women can think it is easier to 'fake it' rather than let their husband know that what he is doing is just not working for them. They don't want to hurt his feelings. But really, if your husband found out you were 'faking it', he would feel hurt. Work at cultivating open and honest conversations, learn what your partner likes, and seek deeper intimacy.

Initiating Sex

Couples don't usually talk about how to initiate sex. To directly tell your spouse you want to be intimate with them, can feel scary. You could get rejected, and rejection is painful. But if you want to avoid missing each other's bids for intimacy, you will have to be clear with your intentions and direct in what you say.

How do you initiate sex with your spouse? How do you let your spouse know you are in the mood? Do you use words or do you use physical touch? How do you know your spouse is up for some sexy fun? Do you like to initiate sex? Would you like your spouse to initiate more or less? How would you like your partner to initiate? Discuss this with your spouse.

Talking about this can help alleviate misunderstandings. If one partner tries to give signals about wanting sex but their spouse completely misreads it and doesn't respond, then it's easy to feel rejected! Or a partner might feel unwanted because their spouse doesn't initiate at all. Work at having a healthy balance of both partners initiating sex at different times. When you initiate sex, you are telling your spouse that you want them. You desire them. This is such an important message to give them.

As a couple, navigate your sexual desire differences through talking about it. State your intention: Let your partner know you are in the mood for sex, intimacy or connection. Make your bid for sex about connection and desire rather than a sexual release. 'I desire to be close to you' or, 'I desire to express my love for you' or even 'I really want you' can sound more appealing than simply saying, 'I want to have sex.'

Enquire where your spouse is at. Are they in the mood as well? Are they sitting on the fence, happy to go either way, or is it just not the right time for them? Don't assume they are peaking with desire at the same moment and intensity as you are. You can rate your level of sexual desire or willingness for sex on a scale from 1 to 9 with 1 being, 'I'm not interested in sex at all right now and I don't want my mind changed,' to 5 being 'I'm sitting on the fence and can go either way,' to a 9 or 10 which would indicate, 'I am full of desire for you.' When you are sitting on a 5, you can invite your spouse to 'try and get me in the mood.'[1]

Not Right Now . . .

If one person really wants to have sex and the other is not in the mood, or is too busy or tired for sex, what should you do? This is the great tension—navigating sexual desire differences with dignity and respect, compromise and flexibility. Create space in your relationship for each person to have the freedom to say no to a request from their partner, but also be flexible and willing to compromise to meet the needs of the other person.

If you are not up for sex, rather than giving a flat out 'no,' consider options. You may not feel like having intercourse but are open to other ways to connect and be intimate together, such as making your partner feel good sexually, giving a massage, cuddling in bed, or sitting close to each other on the couch.

Offer an alternative time that you will be keen for sex, preferably within twenty-four hours, not next month! Such as 'I'm quite tired tonight, but I would be up for it tomorrow morning.' Rescheduling is much better than a flat-out rejection. When you affirm your spouse by saying something like, 'I love being intimate with you but tonight is not the best time for me,' your spouse still feels loved and wanted.

Make sure you follow through with the alternative time you are offering. If you tell your spouse you are not up for it when they are keen, and say, 'Tomorrow morning will be a good time for me,' it is your

---

[1] J Gottman, The seven principles for making marriage work, Harmony, 2015

responsibility to follow through in the morning. Remember, your spouse is hanging out for the morning! When you follow through on your word, you show your spouse that they are your priority and their needs matter to you. This builds trust in your relationship.

Compliment Each Other

Allow your words to be complimentary and encouraging, not demanding or critical. Never criticise your partner's body! Compliment and admire each other's bodies. Your bodies are created by God, and what He creates, He calls good!

Inspired by The Passion Translation of the Song of Songs, here are some compliments you can give your spouse:

> 'You are so lovely.' (1:5)
>
> 'It is you I long for.' (1:7)
>
> 'You are so beautiful. You are beauty itself to me.' (4:1)
>
> 'You are pleasing beyond words.' (1:16)
>
> 'You are my darling companion. You stand out from all the rest.' (2:2)
>
> 'How satisfying to me, my equal, my bride. Your love is my finest wine—intoxicating and thrilling. And your sweet, perfumed praises—so exotic, so pleasing.' (4:10)
>
> 'There is no one else but you, my friend, my equal.' (5:2)
>
> 'Most sweet are his kisses, even his whispers of love. He is delightful in every way and perfect from every viewpoint. If you ask me why I love him so, O brides-to-be, it is because there is none like him to me. Everything about him fills me with holy desire! And now he is my beloved—my friend forever.' (5:16)

'Turn your eyes from me! I can't take it anymore! I can't resist the passion of these eyes that I adore. Overpowered by a glance, my ravished heart is undone. Held captive by your love, I am truly overcome!' (6:5)

'How delicious is your fair beauty, it cannot be described as I count the delights you bring to me. Love has become the greatest. You stand in victory above the rest, stately and secure as you share with me your vineyard of love.' (7:6-7)

'For your kisses of love are exhilarating, more than any delight I've known before.' (7:9)

'Now I know that I am filled with my beloved and all his desires are fulfilled in me.' (7.10)

The following are some suggested topics you can discuss as a couple over a 4-week period.

Week One: Expectations and Communication

What are your expectations of sex in our marriage? How frequently would you like to have sex? Are you flexible or rigid in the things we do each time?

How can we create comfortable and regular ways to discuss sex?

Do you feel comfortable to share your desire to be intimate with me? How can I help you open up more with me about this? Do you worry you will be rejected if you tell me your wants or desires?

What do you find attractive about me? What is the sexiest part of my body? What part of my body do you love the most? Are there parts of your body that you are self-conscious about? Why?

How can I make you feel more confident in our love making?

How have you felt connected to me this week? What things did I do or say that made us feel close this week?

Have there been times this week where you have desired to be close, physically or emotionally and we have missed each other, or it didn't happen?

Week Two: Preferences

What feels good to you?

What part of our lovemaking do you enjoy the most?

How can I pleasure you more?

Do you prefer sex in the morning or evening?

When we are making love, do you enjoy our erotic sounds and noises or prefer us to be soft and quiet?

What is one thing you would like to try as foreplay?

What type of afterplay would you like to try?

Is there something we can do that can make us feel more connected during sex?

Week Three: Initiating and Desire Differences

What could I do to build your desire for sex?

What should we do if one of us really wants to have sex and the other one is not keen for sex in that moment?

Do you like to initiate sex? Would you like me to initiate more or less? How would you like me to initiate?

How do you initiate sex? What signs do you give me that let me know you are in the mood? Do you prefer to communicate through words, body language, or physical affection?

Should we set up a code word that both of us share with each other as the message that we are in the mood?

Week Four: Spicing it up

What new positions would you like to try together?

Do you have any fantasies about us that you would like to share?

What different things can we try to make our sex life more fun and adventurous? What about costume dress up, games, weekend getaways, twenty-four-hour luxury hotel rooms, or different places?

How can we add variety to our sex life? What do you think about longer lovemaking on the weekends and shorter, more frequent lovemaking during the week?

6.
YOUR SEXUAL JOURNEY
Cultivating great sex together

Sex with the same person gets better over time. It's a beautiful journey of getting to know your spouse and understanding another soul intimately and personally. Doing life together gives couples the opportunity to learn so much more about each other—over the years you start to understand what each other means by what they say, you discover each other's quirks, what makes them feel special, and what makes them mad. You find yourself feeling safe and comfortable in each other's presence as each partner let their inhibitions go, and you learn to be vulnerable and silly, to play and laugh with each other. From a secure place in your relationship, knowing you are loved and accepted, you can relax in each other's presence and be confident to explore and try new things together. Unconditional love is powerful and freeing.

THE STAGES OF LIFE

Marriage takes a couple through many different seasons of life. There is the exciting season of becoming a newlywed, the romantic wedding, the honeymoon, and setting up your home and life together. Then the season of pregnancy and children brings beauty, new life and joy into your home. During this stage of life, lack of sleep, long hours of caring for children, and the unending demands of caring and cleaning, can give you only the slightest, rarest opportunity for uninterrupted time together.

As children grow and go to school, however, this changes; family demands are still high as children participate in more extra-curriculum activities, yet their growing independence means they can be in front of a television on their own while you can lock the door for some couple time—hopefully uninterrupted! There may be times in your marriage when you need to dig deep to build your business, work through infertility or health challenges, navigate seasons of financial or emotional stress, or care for aging parents. As we go through life, there are more demands on our time and attention!

Peter and Julia enjoyed a satisfying sex life early in their marriage. But as Julia's parents started aging, her attention turned to them, bringing a lot of stress to her life. Peter got made redundant after twenty years in the same company, and it made him start questioning his life's purpose. This impacted their sex life. Peter started to not be able to sustain his erections and Julia took it personally, thinking he wasn't attracted to her anymore. She questioned her confidence, and his love for her. They couldn't seem to talk about it as both partners would react strongly and defensively. The life stresses this couple were going through brought tension to their marriage bed.

Every season is an opportunity for your sexual journey together to be a place of fun, safety, comfort and play time. I often tell couples that kids get to go to the park for play time, to 'let off steam, get their sillies out, laugh, play imaginary games with others, and have fun.' But what about couples? Couples need play time too! Your sex life can be the place where you come together, let go of the cares of the world for a moment, and allow yourselves to play. With sex, you can let your inhibitions go, laugh, be silly and have fun with each other. Your sexual intimacy is the fun, stress-releasing part of your relationship. No one enjoys a serious, rigid and stressful sexual relationship.

Ben and Sarah were very attracted to each other when they were dating. There was so much sexual energy between them, they couldn't keep their hands off each other! Their faith convictions kept them waiting for sex until they were married. When they got married, they were so excited to enjoy sexual bliss with each other. It took some time to figure out how to enjoy each other and how to make it fun for each other, but they enjoyed pleasurable sex.

Then Sarah got pregnant and over the next five years they had three kids together. Soon, Ben and Sarah found their sex life had dwindled. There was less time for each other as kids, careers, housework and family took up a lot of their energy and mental capacity. They didn't really talk about this change with each other, but silently hoped it was just a stage and that things would get better. However, as life got busier, they had even less time for each other. They couldn't find the time or effort to go out on date nights.

Fast forward twenty years . . . the kids have moved out of home and now Ben and Sarah find themselves on their own with each other, and lonely. When they go to bed, they give each other a kiss, say good night and roll over to sleep. It's almost like a 'high-five, love you!' but there is no passion, intimacy or sexual tension between them.

WHEN YOU FEEL 'STUCK'

No one gets married thinking they will end up in a sexless relationship. We get married with high hopes and great expectations that our marriage will be full of chemistry, connection, fun, play and intimacy. And we should! Jesus came to give us life in abundance!

As the years go on, our sexual intimacy and our sexual functioning can look different or change in different ways—we may experience sexual dysfunction, desire discrepancy, or painful sex. We may become so consumed with life that we are too busy for sex. There may even be unresolved conflict in our relationship, creating resentment and blocking our intimacy and vulnerability. We may have unresolved trauma from past abuse or unmet emotional, physical or sexual needs that we handle through unhealthy behaviours, habits or addictions. The last thing a couple wants to become is unhappy, discontent housemates.

There will be times when a couple feels stuck, not knowing how to move forward. They can start to interpret their sexual problems as meaning, 'we are no longer sexually compatible.' But this does not have to be the case. You are only sexually incompatible when you stop working at your sex life and your marriage.

Sexual intimacy is such an important part of marriage. You can have a great marriage and a great sex life! You don't need to settle for one or the other. It will take work and there may be times when you don't feel like putting each other first or when you don't desire each other. In those moments, it requires intention to choose your marriage and give it priority. The seemingly insignificant, daily moments of being open, caring and affectionate to each other and not taking each other for granted is an investment. Commit to continually working through any issues or challenges that come up in your sex life and relational intimacy.

At the start of your marriage, you can decide together to build a great sex life for the years to come. Let's explore some keys to cultivating great sex together.

Keep Touching

Always make physical affection a part of your relationship. Holding hands, sharing a kiss, giving each other a hug . . . these should be a regular and consistent way of showing each other affection in public and at home. It's a way of showing love, care and comfort, and it should not always have an agenda of 'let's have sex' attached to it. The beautiful thing about physical affection is that when we share it with someone, we feel safe, secure and connected, and that in turn triggers a release of oxytocin. Oxytocin relieves stress, lowers blood pressure and gives you feelings of trust, connection, bonding and contentment.[1]

When physical affection is only given when you are interested in sex, it limits each partner's ability to freely express their affection for one another. Maybe he wants to simply enjoy caressing your buttocks? Maybe she needs a hug to calm down from a stressful day? Maybe she wants to simply kiss you because you look so handsome in that suit? You don't want your partner to feel like they need to hold back their devotion to you or their desire to touch and be close to you out of worry or fear that it will give the wrong impression. The reality is that not every affectionate touch means 'I want to have sex with you!' You need to make sure there are ample opportunities to express your love for each other in ways that are not just an invitation to be sexual.

If you do find your marriage is in a season where sexual intimacy is challenged, make sure that you continue to place importance on your physical affection. There are many non-sexual, intimate things you can do together to build your connection and intimacy.

Prioritise Sex

Life gets busy and sex can end up being the last thing on your mind. Don't let your sexual intimacy become the last item on your long to-do-list or the last thing you do before going to sleep. Your spouse should not always get your tired leftovers from the day. They can also have you at your best!

Prioritising sex involves planning for sex. So many people get stuck on the thought that they should not have to plan for sex. It messes

---

[1] For further reading, see S Kuchinskas, The Chemistry of Connection: How the oxytocin response can help you find trust, intimacy, and love, New Harbinger Publications, 2009

with their expectations of what they think sex should be like. Shouldn't sex be spontaneous? Isn't sex meant to be filled with irresistible passion? Doesn't sex just happen?

Remember, the movies have lied to us! Sex in the movies shows highly passionate and erotic moments where clothes are ripped off each other in a heighted quest to get to each other's bodies, followed by both partner's experiencing simultaneous orgasms as soon as they touch each other. As unrealistic as it sounds, these sex scenes in movies still give us the impression that sex is naturally impulsive, animalistic and does not need planning.

Sex in the movies, however, is not the same as in real life. In a long-term, committed relationship where both partners are balancing a lot of life's plates at the same time, sex may require a bit of planning. The most exciting, fun things in life, like a holiday, don't just happen impulsively—they happen because they are planned. It's the same with sex—whether you schedule it into your week, book a luxury hotel, or arrange to send the kids to their grandparents, you are planning for sex. This also means you have time to look forward to it, to think and imagine what it will be like, and this anticipation is the best kind of foreplay.

Invent and re-invent ways to put your relationship first. Prioritising each other involves creating time for just the two of you. It is so easy to take each other for granted and to become familiar, especially as the years go by. It can also be easier to deny that there is a problem or to avoid the difficulties when your relationship feels stuck.

If you feel you are becoming distant or growing apart, be brave enough to arrest it by coming back to each other, talking through the challenges, and rearranging your priorities to keep each other up there as number one.

When your work schedules are different, or one of you is a morning person while the other is a night owl, make it a priority to either go to sleep or wake up at the same time. If you can't do that on weekdays, at least try to make it work on weekends so that you don't become 'ships passing through the night.' One way to work with the 'early riser, night owl' situation is for the 'night owl' to put the 'early riser' to bed. And, if you can't sleep in the same bed due to snoring, be sure to spend time each day connecting and being intimate.

Stay Curious

How curious are you about your spouse? Sexual boredom only happens when you stop being curious. How well do you actually know your spouse? As onions have many layers, people also have many layers. We never truly know everything about a person. When we get comfortable in our partner's presence, we can easily settle with what we already know about them. But this stops us being curious. There is always so much more to know about your spouse!

Curiosity is leaving what you already know to discover more about your spouse, their body, their vulnerability, their pleasure and your intimacy together. There is so much to delight in! Do you look at your spouse with curiosity? Do you have a strong desire to know him or her more? Curiosity leads to a creative and imaginative sex life, so stay curious and choose to continually delight in each other!

Create Variety

A couple's sex life can fall into a routine that is boring, non-adventurous and bland. This predictable type of sex is commonly referred to as a couple's 'sex script.' It is predictable because the couple knows exactly how their lovemaking goes—'a quick kiss, a rubbing touch and then into intercourse,' for example. The lack of effort invested in creating variety and adventure can be masked by excuses: 'I have a headache,' or 'I'm too tired' or rolling away when your partner reaches for a late-night kiss.

You don't have to default to missionary position every time! Creating variety keeps your sex life exciting and fresh. Sex does not have to be 'the same-old, same-old' routine that a lot of couples fall into. It does not have to be the last thing you do before you go to sleep, nor does it always have to be a long-winded event charged with expectation, planning and anticipation.

When you are familiar with each other's bodies, you know each other's 'short cuts,' what turns them on and gets them aroused quickly. And because there are times when you don't have the energy or time for a long, drawn-out 'banquet session,' a 'quickie' can keep it fun and keep you both connected.

When you have children and teenagers around, being alone is a rare luxury. It can be fun and exciting to look for times to seize the moment and take the chance to be intimate while your kids are out at soccer practice or downstairs watching a movie or awake talking to their friend in their room. The excitement and rush of keeping quiet, not being caught and being quick, can keep sex fun in the seasons when your uninterrupted 'free time' is limited. Flexibility and being adaptable allows your sexual journey together to be fresh and exciting.

Sex is like drinking coffee. Sometimes you only have time for a takeaway coffee; other days you can sit down for fifteen minutes, and sometimes you can spend hours sitting and chatting over multiple cups of coffee. You can enjoy the same thing in different ways. Long sex sessions, quick sessions, and playful sessions all nurture your couple intimacy.

There are so many ways a couple can have a healthy and mutually satisfying sex life. Stir up your imagination and get creative! Don't get rigid and locked in about what sex should be like every time. Create variety and keep things fun by being adaptable, flexible and creative in the season you are in together. And whenever you are unsure, reflect on the following questions inspired by Sexologist Patricia Weerakoon and discuss them as a couple:[2]

Respect and Honour—Does this value and honour my spouse and our marriage? Does it build trust? Does it show respect? Does it objectify or degrade my spouse? Am I treating my spouse the way I would treat my own body?

Safety—Does this make both of us feel safe and secure in our relationship? Is there a possibility this activity could harm me or my spouse physically or emotionally?

Connection—Does this enhance our marriage relationship? Does it foster connection with each other in mind and body? Does this bring us emotionally and physically closer?

Honour Each Other

Everything we do sexually together should be in line with God's plan for sex, to build intimacy, connection and mutual pleasure. This honours God and causes your marriage to shine for Jesus. Sexual intimacy can either draw two people closer together or it can be a wedge that draws them apart. Ensure both partners are comfortable and consent to what you are considering. Respect your partner if they

---

[2] P Weerakoon, The Best Sex For Life, Growing Faith, 2013

are uncomfortable. Doing something that makes them feel uncomfortable or disrespected will not build your intimacy.

Remember there are two people in your sexual relationship. Marriage is not a 'free access to sex' card allowing us to have all our sexual desires and fantasizes fulfilled. The bible tells us that we are no longer our own. Honour God with your body. He paid a great price for you.

> 'Do you not know that your bodies are temples of the Holy Spirit, who is in you, whom you have received from God? You are not your own; you were bought at a price. Therefore, honor God with your bodies.' 1 Corinthians 6.19-20 NIV

Forgive Often

Nothing can keep a couple out of the bedroom like unforgiveness, bitterness and resentment. Forgiveness is your most powerful weapon in your battle to maintain unity with each other. Psalm 133:1 says that, 'Where there is unity, God commands a blessing.'

Forgiveness is not feelings-based; it is not dependant on whether you feel like forgiving your partner. Forgiveness is a choice, a powerful choice indeed. Forgiveness disarms the hurt, offense or disappointment, and annuls its power over you. When you stay in unforgiveness, resentment grows, which causes you to turn further and further from each other. This only causes more hurt and pain.

A husband can be broken by his wife not wanting him, and a wife can be broken by her husband not wanting her. Shutting down from each other, emotionally, physically and sexually, harms you both.

'Addressing conflict,' on the other hand, 'is the ordinary, day-to-day process through which you can deepen your intimacy.'[3]

> *'Love overlooks the mistakes of others but dwelling on the failures of others devastates friendships.'* Proverbs 17.9 TPT

Note however, that this does not mean that you should simply forgive your partner and stay in an abusive or unsafe relationship. If your personal safety and wellbeing is at risk, get professional help immediately and seek safety from your relationship.

Allow Sex to Bring Healing

Sex can be restorative. It can be reassuring after a disappointment, soothing after a bad day or a welcome distraction during a difficult time. Sex can be a great stress release, a way of bringing safety and belonging to each other when times are scary and uncertain.

Sex can be a 'reset button' in your relationship. Have you ever had days when you just 'rub each other up the wrong way,' days when you bicker and disagree over silly, stupid things like forgetting to take the garbage out, or days where you keep getting on each other's nerves and you 'snap' over nothing? Do you have days when everything your partner does annoys you?

On those days, sex can be like a 'reset button.' Physical touch and intimate pleasure can allow you to let go of the negative tension you have both created or allowed into your relationship and reconnect towards each other. After intimacy, you may find that the tension has left your relationship and you are able to deal with the problem with a clearer

---

[3] B McCarthy, Coping with Erectile Dysfunction: How to Regain Confidence and Enjoy Great Sex, New Harbinger Publications, 2004, p. 99.

mind. Once you have reconnected as a couple, the petty little things that were ticking you off might no longer feel like they are a deal breaker.

Sex by no means is a way of avoiding relationship problems, but it does give couples the opportunity to reset their relationship when they have gone off track and tended toward disunity.

As you embark on your journey of cultivating great sex together, remember and remind each other that your goal and reward is your relationship intimacy.

- Discussion Questions for Couples -

What time could we set aside each week for sex chats?

What type of physical touch brings comfort and connection to you?

What part of my body do you love to touch the most? How curious are you to learn more about me?

What are we communicating to each other during foreplay?

What new position or sexual act, would you like to try?

What is your favourite way to kiss me? How do you like me to kiss you?

How does looking into each other's eyes bring us closer together?

How does it feel to see me experience pleasure, and to let me see yours?

How can we resolve our problems in a way that feels good to both of us? How can sex bring healing and restoration in our marriage?

7.
HONOUR YOUR INTIMACY
Safeguarding your sex life

> *'Honor marriage and guard the sacredness of sexual intimacy between wife and husband.'* Hebrews 13.4 MSG

Honour is defined as 'having high respect or holding great esteem for something or someone.'[1]

Intimacy is a gift in your marriage to cherish, to hold in high respect as something of value and importance in your relationship. As much as we need to cultivate our intimacy, we also need to protect it. The intimacy you have in your marriage is a powerful force, an example to others. Don't take it for granted. Broken intimacy has the potential to cause hurt, pain and destruction to your relationship and to others.

The book of Proverbs has wise advice:

> *'My son, share your love with your wife alone . . . why would you have sex with a stranger or with anyone other than her? Reserve this pleasure for you and her alone and not with another . . . continually delighted and ravished with her love!*
>
> *My son, why would you be exhilarated by an adulteress—by embracing a woman who is not yours? For God sees everything you do and his eyes are wide open as he observes every single habit you have.'* Proverbs 5.15-21 TPT

Young couples in love have eyes only for each other—and, they can't keep their hands off each other. They are intoxicated with love for each other, so much so that it is difficult to imagine anything that could get in the way of this good thing! But for something so good to *stay good*, it needs to be honoured, upheld and valued by both partners, and the marriage bed must be a place that is guarded and protected.

---

[1] https://www.lexico.com/en/definition/honor

There are sexual behaviours or practices that can destroy intimacy and cause relational pain, and it is important, as a newly married couple, that you are aware of them and talk about them in your marriage. One of the biggest 'intimacy-stealers' is pornography.

PORNOGRAPHY

Pornography is defined as 'sexually explicit media intended to sexually excite and arouse the audience. This includes images of nudity, semi-nudity, implied and actual sexual activity.'[2] The goal of pornography is to engage the viewer in a sexual relationship with it.[3]

Although pornography was once assumed to only be a 'male issue,' this is no longer the case. It is designed to appeal to, and target, both men and women. And, it is everywhere—there are websites, online chat rooms, sexually-explicit television shows, explicit games and erotic literature, as well as an abundance of amateur videos depicting real couples involved in sexual activities. The reality is that most people will be exposed to pornography at some stage—more often than not, as an adolescent or even as a child. The average age of first exposure is less than eleven years old.

For many people, exposure to pornography first happened by stumbling across it, often 'by accident.' Others were introduced to it by someone else, generally someone older than them. So often, we hear people say things like:

> 'I found my dad's (or uncle's, or brother's) stash of
> magazines one day and I was intrigued.'

---

[2] M Flood, 'Youth, Sex, and the Internet,' Counselling, Psychotherapy, and Health, Vol. 5 No. 1, 2009, pp.131-147.
[3] W Maltz & L Maltz, The Porn Trap: the essential guide to overcoming problems caused by pornography, HarperCollins, 2008.

'I wasn't looking for it, but it popped up on my computer.'

'I clicked on a link from social media of a girl in a bikini and it took me to images I wasn't even looking for.'

'My friend showed me pictures from their phone.'

For some people, stumbling across pornography or being introduced to it by someone else sparked a curiosity in them. For others, their own desire led them to seek pornography for themselves. However it happened, for many young people today, pornography is their prominent form of sex education.

It is normal to be curious and feel excited about sexual behaviour. Curiosity can create an interest in pornography which fades over time; more likely, though, the 'sparked interest' develops into a regular occurrence, often developing into a habit and for some, into an addiction that becomes difficult to stop.

> **Talk together:**
>
> *Have you watched or been exposed to pornography at some stage in your life? Is pornography currently part of your life?*

As much as pornography has become normalised in our culture, we need to understand how destructive it is to a person's sexual development and intimate relationships.

Pornography creates unhealthy beliefs, gives inaccurate depictions of the type of sex people enjoy, and misrepresents how partners like to be treated in sex. Pornography teaches us that sex is pleasurable when it is hard, intense and fast. It promotes unrealistic expectations about how a woman experiences orgasm and what a sexually intimate relationship looks like—it does not teach or model safe-sex practices, consent or respect. There is nothing in pornography that depicts intimacy, communication, compassion and care for each other.

And yet, this inaccurate depiction of sex is the only perception many people have about sex. Pornography has taught generations of young people what sex is, what sexual acts are like, and how to interact with sexual partners. The problem is, the education we have received from pornography is unhealthy and destructive.

For a start, pornography requires no effort on the user's behalf. You don't need an imagination when you have porn. You don't need to explore a person's body or take the time to know someone intimately. Pornography doesn't allow you to talk to your partner or find out what they like—it simply teaches that sex is 'all about me, my self-gratification and my self-pleasure.'

Bringing a pornographic mindset to marriage destroys trust and affects your sexual intimacy. There is no way to indulge in pornography without it affecting your spouse and your intimacy in marriage. The reality is, that as sex becomes quick and transactional, the relational and emotional connection is lost, and sex is reduced to simply being about sexual release. But sex is so much more than this!

What makes pornography so destructive, is that it essentially rewires your brain, until having healthy sex with another real-life person seems boring and unexciting. Over time, it can lead you to become dependent on visual imagery for sexual arousal, which can result in the inability to be sexually aroused or maintain an erection with a real-life partner. This sexual dysfunction is called 'porn-induced erectile dysfunction'. With the significant increase in recent years of erectile dysfunction, delayed ejaculation, unmet sexual expectations, sexual dissatisfaction and low sexual desire during partnered sex in young men, there is convincing research to support the connection between pornography and erectile dysfunction.[4]

To address the issue, we need to consider why you or your spouse feel drawn to pornography. It is not just a 'bad habit.' It is a quick-fix approach to 'feeling good' when boredom, loneliness, stress, depression, anxiety or a sense of inadequacy has taken over. It always seems easier to use pornography to help yourself feel better, than to address the root of the issue.

Getting married will not fix a porn problem

Most people wish they had more power over their habit, compulsion or addiction to pornography, and the danger comes in thinking that marriage will be the answer. So many people think, 'when I get married, I will stop looking at porn,' only, it rarely works out that way.

The reality is that pornography is destructive to your spouse. A husband or wife can end up feeling responsible, or pressured. 'If I just give him (or her) more sex, their porn issue will be fixed' or, 'if I do some sexual act even though I'm not comfortable with it, their sexual fantasy problem will stop.' Then, when they find their partner is continuing to use pornography or is masturbating, defeat can set in, and the husband or wife is left wondering, 'what is wrong with me?' or 'am I not good enough for him/her?'

If your husband or wife is addicted to pornography, you need to know that their habit is not your responsibility to fix. And if you struggle with pornography, you need to recognise that your problem will only be fixed when you recognise your need for help and reach out for it.

---

[4] Park, Brian Y et al. "Is Internet Pornography Causing Sexual Dysfunctions? A Review with Clinical Reports." Behavioral sciences (Basel, Switzerland) vol. 6,3 17. 5 Aug. 2016, doi:10.3390/bs6030017

Now is the best time to be brave. You can never be completely vulnerable and intimate with your spouse if you are hiding things from each other. You need to bring it into the light.

How can I fix a porn problem?

The first thing you can do is to block your ability to access porn. Install software protection on all your devices so that you are unable to search for pornography. If you are viewing pornography on social media, YouTube or websites, delete the apps or accounts and give the password to someone you trust to reset so you can't reinstall the apps or reopen your account when you feel tempted to view.

Secondly, renew your mind by developing a healthy view on sexuality. You can do this by reading about healthy sexuality and sexual relationships, listening to Godly teaching and wise counsel about sex, and observing the healthy relationships that are modelled around you.

Thirdly, start to understand the sort of things that trigger your use of porn and address those, preferably with a trusted friend, professional counsellor or Pastor. Build transparency into your friendships and practice vulnerability, safety and honesty in those friendships. Although pornography rewires your brain, Jesus gives us the power to renew our minds. It's a process, but it's never too late to start taking back your mind and heart . . . and your sexual life!

Is pornography okay if we are both fine with it?

The simple answer is, no. Pornography gives an inaccurate depiction of healthy sex. It turns your attention away from your spouse and takes your focus away from your intimacy and connection. When you view pornography, you allow other people into your sexual relationship, when God designed it to for just the two of you as husband and wife. Your sexual intimacy in marriage should not have to compete with pornography.

Ask yourselves why you, as a couple, are using pornography? Is it because you want to learn more about sex and how to bring each other pleasure? If so, get hold of books and resources that have been produced by sexual health experts! This is the best way to get accurate information—and then, you can have fun putting it all into practice as you explore and experiment with each other's bodies in *real life*.

Perhaps you are viewing pornography as a couple in order to help with stimulation and arousal. If so, you need to know that real life stimulation will never be able to compete and compare to the hyper-stimulation and arousal that pornography can give. If you want to provide more stimulation, arousal and satisfaction to each other, put in some work! Connect, engage, and explore each other's bodies. Great sex takes effort and time; it requires patience and curiosity. And be assured that when you put in the effort required to understand how to satisfy your spouse, it will bring a great reward to you both, and your sex life *will* get better!

MASTURBATION

Masturbation can be self-exploring, tension-releasing and self-soothing; many normalise it as a natural part of our sexual development. Masturbation is part of our inner world and is the one sexual act that we don't often talk openly about, especially with our spouse. We tend to assume that masturbation is not necessary in marriage because, of course, you have each other! But communicating about masturbation in your marriage is essential to building intimacy.

What makes masturbation destructive, painful and divisive, is when it is hidden away and done in secret. Exploring your body in your partner's presence, however, can enable both of you to learn about touch and pleasure while building connection and intimacy. Some people may not feel comfortable exploring their body in their partner's presence, so if, as a couple, you decide to self-explore your body on your own to start with, be transparent and open in your communication. Tell each other when you are doing it, how you felt and what you learned about your body so that your partner is included in the process.

> **Talk together:**
>
> *As a couple, what do you think about self-exploration, especially when you are new at all this 'sex stuff' and are trying to figure out how your body works? Would you both be happy if one partner self-explores on their own? How long will you do this for before you come back and explore each other together?*

Fred's wife, Jane, goes on regular business trips. She heads up a department in a global company that requires her to travel overseas regularly. Sometimes Fred and Jane are apart for up to a month at a time. This is really hard on them, both relationally and sexually, and although they videocall each other several times a day to stay connected, the distance between them leaves Fred feeling sexually frustrated. Fred and Jane want to know if there is a place for masturbation in their marriage, while they are apart?

As a couple, talk about your sexual intimacy when circumstances keep you apart, whether this is because of a business trip, chronic illness, or issues related to childbearing. Do you want masturbation to be among your sexual options as a couple? If so, talk about when this would be acceptable to you, and if you would like your partner to masturbate in your presence or alone.

God designed sex to be a shared experience. Masturbation has the potential to destroy your intimacy when it is hidden from your spouse or used as a replacement for your spouse. Masturbation can also be a form of sexual avoidance, a distancing behaviour that satisfies your own sexual desire . . . solo.

It is easy to avoid sex with your spouse when you have satisfied your own needs, but this damages your relationship and communicates rejection to your spouse. It is very hard to *not* take it personally when a husband or wife does not want to make love, yet willingly turns to masturbation.

Think carefully about the *why* behind the act. Masturbation may be self-satisfying for a moment, but does it benefit your relationship? Does it keep you faithful to your spouse in your mind? Are you using masturbation to make you feel better when you are lonely, bored or emotionally low? Does it feel easier to masturbate than to be with your spouse? Is it a habit that you can't control or don't want to stop? Does it produce feelings of guilt and shame, causing you to retreat, distance yourself, or be dishonest with your spouse? Does masturbation build your emotional bond with each other?

Remember, anything that does not add to your emotional and physical intimacy will, in fact, take away from the intimacy you have built in your relationship.

> **Talk together:**
>
> Are there circumstances or seasons where you would use masturbation personally? Are you comfortable with masturbating when you are together? Are you comfortable for one partner to masturbate if the other partner is not keen for sex or if you are apart for a while? Would you like your partner to tell you when they masturbate? If your partner feels they need to masturbate, would you like them to tell you so you can meet their needs instead?

SEX TOYS

'I've been using a vibrator while we have intercourse. I find it really helps me achieve orgasm. Is this bad? Does using sex toys make our marriage bed impure?'

Sex toys increase and hasten arousal through intense stimulation. They can spice up a dull sex life, increase pleasure and enhance your fun together. Sex toys can also be helpful when a couple are learning what an orgasm feels like or are exploring ways to build arousal. A woman may choose to use a vibrator to get aroused quickly, then invite her husband to bring her to orgasm. A vibrator can also be useful when you are having a 'quickie' so both partners have a chance to orgasm. [5]

Sex toys can be used to create emotional, spiritual and sexual intimacy. However, be careful that they do not make your sexual intimacy feel impersonal or performance-focused, much like pornography. Although sex toys can provide quick, intense

---

[5] L Watson, Wanting Sex Again: How to rediscover your desire and heal a sexless marriage, Berkley, 2012

stimulation, it is way more delightful to experience the soft loving touch of your partner's hands and lips.

Sex toys should never be used as a replacement for you! If you do not know how to stimulate your partner or build your arousal or bring your husband or wife to orgasm, using a sex toy can be the 'lazy' option. Better to have the patience and be willing to learn, so that your spouse truly feels valued and important.

SEXUAL FANTASY

God is creative! He created the world and formed you in His image. He placed creativity and imagination within you; it is a God-given gift. Cultivating sexual imagination can powerfully build your 'couple eroticism' and enhance your sexual relationship. Sexual fantasies are often about high levels of energy, eroticism and engagement by both partners. It is a brave and vulnerable move to allow your spouse into your inner world of imagination! Discussing each other's fantasies might give you fresh ideas about what you can do together to build a sex life that is fun, exciting and spicy!

Sexual imagination and fantasy can enhance your sexual desire. Daydream about what you will do together later that night or on that romantic getaway, relive your favourite memories with each other in your mind, and activate fantasy, your sexual imagination, in order to arouse your body and build your responsiveness for sex. Then, when your partner reaches for you, or when you come home after a big day, you will be ready and willing to turn towards each other in your bid for intimacy and connection.

It is empowering to activate your sexual imagination and see how it can enhance your sexual relationship. This is the positive side of sexual fantasy—when it is about you and your spouse and is used to build anticipation, intimacy and connection. Remember though, that fantasies do not have to be lived out. It is not your right or your partner's responsibility to fulfil your every fantasy and desire. It is also unrealistic to expect that you will fulfil your spouse's every sexual desire or fantasy (although if you want to try, go ahead!). If you are comfortable with entering into each other's fantasies, ensure that you can stop at any time. Never play along out of pressure or obligation, as this could be detrimental to your emotional and physical safety as well as your intimacy and connection as a couple.

If you create your own fantasy during sexual intimacy, consider whether it is because you are not adequately aroused or are feeling disconnected from your spouse. If so, talk about it together and explore ways to build arousal and connection in your relationship. It could be that working on the connection and excitement aspect of your sexual intimacy will bring the stimulation and satisfaction that you hoped to achieve through personal fantasy.

The key with sexual fantasy is to exercise self-control. Your fantasies are not conducive to building your couple intimacy if the fantasy involves someone aside from your spouse. It may appear harmless since no one else knows what you are thinking, but it does not build faithfulness to your spouse when you indulge in fantasies about someone else.

Entertaining sexual fantasies is a choice, and you must be clear that a fantasy that is centred on anyone other than your spouse, whether it is a person at the gym or a colleague in your office, is not innocent. Fantasising about someone else does not honour and respect your spouse and it will compromise your ability to stay faithful.

Remember, temptation does not go away simply because you are married. If you find yourself attracted to, or sexually desiring, someone that is not your spouse or even fantasising about someone else while you are being sexually intimate with your spouse, you are on dangerous ground. Unfaithfulness starts in the mind before it becomes a behaviour. Sexual desire requires self-control.

> 'May your fountain be blessed, and may you rejoice in the wife of your youth. A loving doe, a graceful deer, may her breasts satisfy you always, may you ever be intoxicated with her love.' Proverbs 5:18-19 NIV

You are called to love the person God has given you with all your heart, mind and soul. Jesus says,

> 'This is my commandment: "Love each other in the same way I have loved you."' John 15:12 NLT

So focus your attention on your spouse, and learn to enjoy, delight in, and fall in love with your spouse, over and over again.

- Discussion Questions for Couples -

What can we do to safeguard our intimacy?

Have you watched or been exposed to pornography at some stage in your life? Is pornography currently part of your life?

Do you think masturbation should have a role within our marriage?

Are there circumstances where you would personally like to use masturbation?

Are you comfortable with masturbation if one of us is not keen for sex or if we are apart?

What do you think about using sex toys in our marriage? Could they be beneficial? Why or why not?

Do you have sexual fantasies that you would like us to explore as a couple? Do those fantasies build a stronger connection between us?

A PERSONAL PRAYER FOR YOUR SEXUALITY

Thank you, God, that You are the God of Intimacy and the Creator of Sex, and that You have created me with the desire for intimacy and connection. Thank you that You are my safe place; you welcome me into Your open arms with a warm smile and kindness in your eyes. I can be vulnerable with You and let You close.

There is no shame in Your presence and no condemnation for those in Christ Jesus. In Your presence is where I belong, where I am known, affirmed and accepted. I am safe, I am seen, I am loved and I am enough. You are the one who makes me whole. You are the only One who can meet all my needs and make me complete, and I invite You to meet all my needs and make me whole.

I choose to honour You with my sexuality, God, in my marriage and in my relationships. I invite You, Holy Spirit, to restore and heal my heart and to renew my mind about Your plan for my sexuality. Help me to see and understand sex the way You created it.

I pray that our marriage will be a safe place where both of us can be who we really are with each other, a place to enjoy each other's sexuality to the fullest. I declare that our sexual intimacy will be a gift for each of us to enjoy, that it will enhance our unity and connection and that this part of our relationship will bring You glory.

Help us to honour and cherish the gift of our sexuality and may we model to others, that healthy, God-honouring sex in marriage is the very best!

Amen.

- RECOMMENDED READING -

Come As You Are: *The surprising new science that will transform your sex life*, by Emily Nagoski

Coping with Erectile Dysfunction: *How to regain confidence and enjoy great sex*, by Barry McCarthy

Daring Greatly: *How the courage to be vulnerable transforms the way we live, love, parent, and lead*, by Brené Brown

Hold Me Tight, by Dr Sue Johnson

Intended for Pleasure, by Ed and Gaye Wheat

Love Sense: *The revolutionary new science of romantic relationships*, by Dr Sue Johnson

Passionate Marriage: *Keeping love and intimacy alive in committed relationships*, by David Schnarch

She Comes First: *The thinking man's guide to pleasuring a woman*, by Ian Kerner

Sheet Music, by Dr Kevin Leman

The Best Sex for Life, by Patricia Weerakoon

The Seven Principles for Making Marriage Work, by John Gottman

The Sexual Healing Journey: *A guide for survivors of sexual abuse*, by Wendy Maltz

Wanting Sex Again: *How to rediscover your desire and heal a sexless marriage*, by Laurie Watson

Where Did My Libido Go? by Rosie King

- ABOUT THE AUTHOR -

Renee Yam is an esteemed sexologist, counsellor and speaker who specialises in sex, intimacy, and relationships. Renee is passionate about educating people about God's design and plan for sex and equipping them to experience in fullness, a healthy and Godly sexuality.

Renee Yam has professional affiliations with Australian Counselling Association and Society of Australian Sexologists. She has a Bachelor of Economics from the University of Sydney, a Postgraduate Diploma in Social Health from Macquarie University and a Master of Health Science (Sexual Health) from the University of Sydney.

Renee loves building the local church, and has over 15 years' experience working in churches, leadership teams and pastoral counselling settings. She has also developed a range of successful community-based initiatives for groups and individuals, focussing on personal development, sexual health and relationships.

Renee has her own private counselling practice, where she specialises in providing relationship and sex therapy to people of all demographics. She believes each person has intrinsic value and desires to draw out people's strengths and help them discover the potential within them. She lives in Sydney, Australia with her husband and family.

- THANK YOU -

This book would not have been possible without the many people who have invested into my life personally and professionally, and the people who have bravely shared their stories with me over the years. Thank you is not enough. I dedicate this book to you all.

To my mentor, **Dr Patricia Weerakoon**. Your life's work in the sexology field has been an inspiration to me. Thank you for the years of investment of your time, knowledge and encouragement. Your consistent belief in me is why I am doing what I'm doing, and your mentorship has truly been a gift from God in my life.

To my Pastors, **Brian and Bobbie Houston**. Thank you for building a church where I found the God of Intimacy for myself. Your empowering leadership has allowed me to lift the lid off my potential and dream big for God.

To my editor, **Anya McKee**. Thank you for your expertise, way with words and time spent working on this book. It's been a breath of fresh air to work with someone who 'gets' my message and believes in it as much as I do.

To my illustrator, **Camille Green**. Thank you for being willing to design my anatomy requests. Your work is truly incredible!

To my husband, **Allen**. You have consistently believed in me and encouraged me when I doubted and questioned myself. I am forever thankful that you are so releasing and proud of the work I do.

To my **girls**. You will all change the world!

- PASS IT ON -

Thank you for reading this book! If this book has helped you, please take a moment to recommend it to others or share it with a friend.

You can also find out more about Renee's work by following her on Facebook and Instagram, or by visiting her website:

www.sexthewholestory.com.au

- sexthewholestory
- @sexthewholestory

For any enquiries, please get in touch at:
info@sexthewholestory.com.au

www.ingramcontent.com/pod-product-compliance
Lightning Source LLC
Chambersburg PA
CBHW070256010526
44107CB00056B/2474